PRAISE FOR *The Soulmate Secret*

"Arielle Ford, in inspiring and encouraging terms, offers from her direct experience how to prepare in consciousness, heart and spirit to magnetize, recognize and respond to the soul's call for an authentic, conscious love relationship."

—Michael Bernard Beckwith, author of *Spiritual Liberation*

"With a harmonious blend of the metaphysical as well as the practical, *The Soulmate Secret* guides you with example after example down the path of finding true love. Arielle gives easy to apply guidance to let go of anything that may keep you from finding the romantic relationship you deserve. If you're looking for love, buy this book—you'll be glad you did."

—James Arthur Ray, author of *Harmonic Wealth*

"As someone who has been studying, practicing and teaching the Law of Attraction for over forty years, I am thrilled to come across a book that so beautifully translates the universal principles of manifestation into an actionable plan for attracting a loving and fulfilling relationship."

—Jack Canfield, author of *Jack Canfield's Key to Living the Law of Attraction*

"*The Soulmate Secret* contains the recipe for love, romance, and unimaginable futures—a recipe that I watched my sister Arielle Ford create and live. With clarity and insight, this book outlines all the ingredients for getting the love that you truly desire and deserve. Read it now, and let the love begin."

—Debbie Ford, author of *Why Good People Do Bad Things*

"To find the love of your life and delight, read this book and manifest the one for you in the sweet now-and-now."

—Mark Victor Hansen, co-creator, *Chicken Soup for the Soul* series

the
soulmate
secret

MANIFEST THE
LOVE OF YOUR LIFE WITH
THE LAW OF ATTRACTION

arielle ford

HarperOne
An Imprint of HarperCollins*Publishers*

HarperOne

HarperCollins books may be purchased for educational, business, or sales promotional use. For information please write: Special Markets Department, HarperCollins Publishers, 10 East 53rd Street, New York, NY 10022.

HarperCollins Web site: http://www.harpercollins.com

HarperCollins®, ☕®, and HarperOne™ are trademarks of HarperCollins Publishers.

FIRST EDITION

Library of Congress Cataloging-in-Publication Data is available upon request.

ISBN 978-0-06-169237-6

09 10 11 12 13 RRD (H) 10 9 8 7 6 5 4 3 2 1

For Brian Hilliard, my soulmate.
You are my rock, my safety net,
my safe place to land, and my springboard
to all that is great about being human.

contents

foreword

Ten years ago I would have loved to have stumbled upon the book you are now holding in your hands!

At that time, I was a forty-year-old single woman with many blessings to count. I was healthy and creatively fulfilled, and my career was thriving. In fact my life was firing on all cylinders except one: I still hadn't found my soulmate. During those years, Arielle (who was then the brilliant publicist for my *Chicken Soup for the Woman's Soul* books) and I spent many long hours on the phone lamenting our plight. Here were two kind, intelligent, passionate, successful women wondering, *Where are all the good men??* If there is such a thing as a "Poor Me" Club, Arielle and I were certainly members in good standing.

Because we talked almost daily, I had a front-row seat to witness the remarkable sequence of events that unfolded as Arielle began applying the powerful Law of Attraction to her love life. The fact that she manifested a loving, supportive, and nurturing relationship with a man as wonderful as Brian certainly inspired me. And her ability to take those timeless principles to the *final frontier*—the domain of intimate relationships—provided a clear blueprint that I followed. One year after Arielle met her soulmate, I met mine.

In the film and book *The Secret*, I shared that most of us have been conditioned to seek outer circumstances like wealth, success, and intimate relationships because we believe those things will make us happy. In fact I've discovered (and wrote about in depth in *Happy for No Reason*) that it's the other way around. The happier we are, the more easily we draw to us everything we want.

Every moment of every day, we are sending out energetic signals that are felt by the people around us. This explains why a desperate person draws to himself or herself more desperation, while a person who is already fulfilled becomes a magnet for greater fulfillment. If we want to attract life partners who are happy, passionate, and empowered, we must first seek to generate these feelings within ourselves.

This is the exact formula Arielle followed with great success in her own life and now prescribes—clearly, practically, and inspirationally—in this book. *The Soulmate Secret* guides you through enjoyable processes and hands-on exercises that help you to savor and celebrate the love you already have in your life, as you prepare yourself on all levels to share that love with another.

As you begin this beautiful journey, I invite you to focus a little less on the happiness you'll extract *from* your soulmate relationship, and a little more on the happiness, love, and contentment you want to bring *to* this relationship. Trust that the timing will be perfect and that, as you fall more deeply in love with yourself, your beloved will be drawn to you like a moth to a flame. See that, know that, feel it all around you, and experience the gratitude as your heart's desire is fulfilled.

With love,
Marci Shimoff

the soulmate IQ test

Answer **YES, NO,** or **NOT SURE** for each question:

Do you believe your soulmate is out there?_____

Are you ready to meet your soulmate today? Right now?_____

If your soulmate had the ability to observe your life right now,
would you be proud of what he or she would see?_____

Are you psychologically and physically in your best condition
to meet your soulmate?_____

Is your home ready to receive your soulmate?_____

Have you made a list of the top ten qualities you want in
your soulmate?_____

Do you regularly exhibit the qualities you believe your
soulmate would find attractive?_____

_____

Are there past lovers who still have their energetic hooks in you—or are yours in them?_____

Are you at peace with the possibility you may never meet your soulmate? (Do you truly believe you'll have a great life even if you never meet that person?)_____

If you answered no to even one of these questions, you may be unconsciously blocking your soulmate from coming into your life. *The Soulmate Secret* will help you remove these blocks and guide you to attract BIG LOVE.

introduction

The minute I heard my first love story,
I started looking for you
not knowing how blind that was.
Lovers don't finally meet somewhere;
they're in each other all along.

Rumi

Have you ever wondered what it takes to meet the love of your life? Is it your dream to find a life partner who will love, cherish, and adore you? If you're longing for a soulmate, this book will show you how to use the Law of Attraction to prepare yourself in body, mind, and soul for the arrival of your beloved.

As someone who didn't meet and marry my soulmate until I was forty-four, I learned a lot along the way about what does and doesn't work in the world of love and romance. I dated controlling men, passive-aggressive men, men who ignored me, and men around whom I felt insignificant and small. In other words, I've been with my share of losers! But I also discovered a formula—what I'm calling the Soulmate Secret—for becoming a magnet for deep and passionate love.

This wonderful Universe of ours is set up to deliver to us the people and experiences that are consistent with our personal belief systems. If you don't believe you will ever find "The One," then guess what? You get to be right . . . you probably won't. If, however, you learn to believe that The One is not only out there but is *also looking for you*, then you open the door for true love to enter.

My grandmother used to say there's a lid for every pot. In other words, there is a match—a perfect partner—for every person. Even so, I have to admit there were many, many times in my thirties when I questioned her theory, because I still hadn't found the lid to my pot. At that point in my life, I was working from home, and the only men I ever met were delivery guys— the mailman, the FedEx guy, the UPS man, the Sparkletts water guy—and most of them were already married!

Then one day I had an experience that really solidified in me the belief that my soulmate was out there . . . somewhere. It happened as I was watching *Oprah* when she had Barbra Streisand on the show. Barbra had recently fallen in love with James Brolin, and I remember thinking, *Here is this super-*

wealthy, ultra famous diva who is "reputedly difficult" and practically inaccessible. How many men could be a match for her? And then I realized, *if the Universe could find somebody for her, then I'll be a piece of cake!* That moment was truly a state of grace. I knew right then with absolute certainty that if the Universe had the perfect man for Barbra Streisand, then my soulmate was definitely out there as well. Still, as the story goes, I had to kiss quite a few frogs before I finally met my prince.

In the early 1980s I was living in Miami, Florida, and dating a very cute but insanely controlling mad scientist. I was sure there had to be some way to change him into a kind, loving, and easy-to-be-with guy. Of course I was very wrong. Trying to make sense of it all, I went for a reading with a notorious Miami Beach psychic. I was sure she was going to tell me just to hang in there and that someday my frog would become a prince and our on-again, off-again relationship would stabilize. Instead, what she said threw me for a loop. She told me that within six months I would be moving to California and that I would spend the rest of my life living along the Pacific Rim. By this point the mad scientist and I had broken up, but I still thought we would get back together (I am *so happy* we didn't—you'll find out why soon enough).

A few weeks later I was unexpectedly fired from my job. I was stunned. I never saw it coming. One of the executives I worked for was surprised to learn I had been fired, and he confided in me that he was also going to resign so he could begin work on a big new project. He told me that in six months he would be able to hire me in what seemed like the perfect job for me. With the security that I had a job waiting for me back in Miami if I wanted it, I felt that this was the perfect time to do something very adventurous. I decided to move to Los Angeles for six months. I had visited L.A. once before and had fallen in love with it. Within days, my bags were packed, and off I went to a city where I had only one friend and no business contacts. On the long airplane ride I read *Creative Visualization* by Shakti Gawain. In it I learned the basic technique of visualizing and feeling the circumstances and events I wanted to manifest into my life. I also read a book called *Key to Yourself*, written in the 1950s by Venice Bloodworth, Ph.D., which offered some very insightful wisdom about prayer and manifestation. In Los Angeles, I attended a New Thought church where I was introduced to a daily prayer to attract abundance into my life. All of these techniques worked!

Within weeks I manifested a good job and the perfect living situation with a roommate, and I made some new friends. Over the next several years, I continued to use this technique to enhance my career and living circumstances, but I just couldn't get it to perform when it came to my love life.

After engaging in some inquiry, going to therapy, and participating in a variety of personal-growth workshops, it finally dawned on me that there were several issues blocking me from manifesting love:

1 I didn't believe I deserved a great relationship.

2 I didn't love myself.

3 I had a lot of emotional baggage.

Until I tackled these things that were holding me back and learned how to specifically adapt the manifestation techniques to something so close to my heart, I wouldn't see the results I wanted. I began using everything I had ever learned about manifestation, psychology, spirituality, and the Law of Attraction and applied it to my love life. My intentions became crystal clear while I simultaneously cleared out the clutter in my home *and* in my heart. I learned and invented techniques, rituals, visualizations, and prayers that helped me prepare my body, mind, heart, spirit, and home for an amazing relationship. And they worked. Within six months of getting serious about manifesting my soulmate, I met my husband, Brian, who has exceeded all my desires and expectations. He was and is everything I ever wished for.

Finding true love is possible for anyone at any age if you're willing to prepare yourself, on all levels, to become an energetic match for the love you're seeking. You have taken an important first step by opening this book. As you immerse yourself in the techniques, rituals, prayers, and projects described on these pages, you will ready yourself in every way to magnetize and meet the man or woman of your dreams. *The Soulmate Secret* is a complete guide for preparing your body, mind, heart, spirit, and home for your perfect life partner.

I am a firm believer that to realize success in any area of our lives, we must balance faith with action. My number one goal is to infuse you with the certainty that your soulmate not only exists but is just as eager to find you as you are to find him or her. And in the meantime there is plenty for you to be doing while you prepare to meet your soulmate, which is why you'll find hands-on, active projects in nearly every chapter.

If you make the space for it, love will find its way to you, and even the most unlikely couplings are possible. Take, for example, the story of Peggy, my mother-in-law. After a fifty-five-year marriage and five years as a widow, Peggy, then eighty years old, set the intention of finding a companion. Within a few months Peggy met John, who had also enjoyed a fifty-plus-year marriage before becoming a widower. Today Peggy and John are like teenagers in love, enjoying the pleasure of rediscovering BIG LOVE in their golden years. Whether you're eighteen or eighty-eight, it's never too late to meet your soulmate.

WHAT IS A SOULMATE?

The term "soulmate" may or may not resonate with you, so let me define exactly what I mean when I use this word. A soulmate is someone with whom you share a deep and profound connection and feel that you can be completely yourself. It's someone whom you love unconditionally and who loves you unconditionally. Without trying to sound too sentimental, a soulmate is someone who "completes" you.

In the movie *Shall We Dance?* starring Richard Gere and Susan Sarandon, there is a terrific scene where Sarandon's character is describing why she loves being married to her soulmate. She says, "We need a witness to our lives. There are a billion people on the planet. . . . I mean, what does any one life really mean? But in a marriage, you're promising to care about everything—the good things, the bad things, the terrible things, the mundane things—all of it, all the time, every day. You're saying, 'Your life will not go unnoticed because I will notice it. Your life will not go unwitnessed because I will be your witness.'" Whether or not you believe in the concept of soulmates, this book will prepare you to manifest the kind of BIG LOVE that Sarandon's character was describing.

DON'T JUST SEE IT; *FEEL* IT

As part of my own process of preparing to meet and manifest my perfect partner, I created a series of processes for myself that I call "feelingizations." While some people might call them visualizations, I think feelingization is the more accurate term. Just being able to visualize isn't enough—you have to *feel* in every cell of your being the outcome you want to create in order to begin to draw it toward you. It's the feeling—not the image—that holds the power to attract.

For example, imagine you want to manifest an expensive luxury car but don't yet know where you'll find the resources. You could visualize every detail of this car and spend days, weeks, or months seeing yourself sitting behind the wheel, *but* if you don't really believe you deserve this car, or if the act of visualizing it conjures more feelings of anxiety than it does of ecstasy, it probably won't happen. You need to be able to *feel* how you will feel driving this car, *knowing* in every cell of your body that you completely deserve it and that at some level it is already yours. This is why I call these processes feelingizations. As you cultivate the feelings you are longing to experience with your soulmate and begin to live as if they were already with you, you will automatically be guided to impulses and actions that will set you upon the path to finding him or her. As a matter of fact, I have used this feelingization technique to navigate almost every major decision I've made in my life.

At the beginning of my career, I didn't always know exactly what I wanted, but I was always sure of how I would feel when I got my heart's desire. For instance, when I moved to Los Angeles in 1984, I needed to manifest a job. Being young and totally new to the entertainment capital of the world, I wasn't at all clear on what kind of job to look for, but I was 100 percent clear that I wanted a job that would leave me feeling satisfied, creative, and well paid. So twice a day I would lie down, close my eyes, and imagine in every part of my body what it would feel like when I had a job that was fun, creative, made good use of my existing skills, and compensated me generously. Within ten days of starting this practice, I found the perfect job. I also used this technique for manifesting a place to live and ended up with not only a

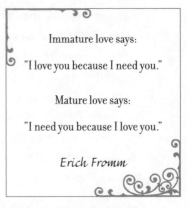

Immature love says:

"I love you because I need you."

Mature love says:

"I need you because I love you."

Erich Fromm

great apartment but a roommate who insisted on doing all the cleaning and cooking!

Prior to meeting Brian, I had a ritual feelingization: Each day at sunset I would light several candles, put on my favorite CD of Gregorian chant, and sit in my big cozy chair. With my eyes closed, I would drop into the feeling of joy of having my soulmate in my life. I would experience these wonderful feelings in every part of my body, knowing even at that moment he was on the way to me (there were days when the thought that he was *very late* did cross my mind, but I would just let those thoughts go and get back to feeling myself in a state of grace and knowing that his arrival was assured).

Feelingizations have the added benefit of being very relaxing, which in turn is good for your health. You can read them to yourself in the quiet moments in the morning and just before going to bed, or if you prefer, you can go to my website,

http://www.soulmatesecret.com/audio and download an audio version of them to listen to at home.

To gain maximum benefit from the feelingizations, I would
suggest that you:

- ✓ *Read* them while lying down or sitting in a comfortable
  chair, in a room where you won't be distracted by people,
  pets, or electronics.

- ✓ *Draw* the shades and light a candle, and if there is a lot of
  outside noise, wear earplugs.

- ✓ *Choose* to do them once a day or once a week; it's completely up to you.

And lastly, if you download the audio versions, PLEASE *please*
do not listen to them while driving. They are intended for use
when you are home and can close your eyes and give them your
undivided attention.

Whether you've been waiting a few months or several years
for your soulmate to arrive, this book will give you the knowledge and tools that will help make your dream of BIG LOVE a
reality.

Let's begin!

Arielle Ford
La Jolla, California

CHAPTER ONE

belief

...

Your task is not to seek for love,
but merely to seek and find
all the barriers within yourself
that you have built against it.

Rumi

Stefanie's Story:
Brokenhearted and Disbelieving

I fell madly in love with someone who I believed with all my heart was The One. We had been friends for fifteen years before we began dating, and we fit together like hand and glove. He was an ambitious Hollywood producer, we were well matched in every way, and we had even started house shopping and discussing marriage. Then I found out he had been having an affair. My heart was so broken that I really thought it might stop beating. I had never cried so much over any breakup, because I really thought he was my soulmate. I decided then and there that all the good men were taken or at least not living in my city—maybe I needed to move? I had a hard time believing I would ever find someone who could really see (and love) all sides of me: the serious career woman, the playful girl, and the tender lover inside of me. I had given up.

[Stay tuned . . . this story has a very happy ending!]

• • •

Stefanie's story echoes what many of us have felt at some point in our lives. After a few (or many) bad relationships, it's so easy to shut down, give up, and stop believing that the right person is out there for us. Our hearts yearn to fall in love, but our minds insist it's not possible, and we enter into a tug-of-war with ourselves. It's as if one part of us is screaming, "Yes! I deserve a great relationship!" while another part insists, "I'll never find him or her." When our beliefs contradict our desires, we experience an inner conflict that not only paralyzes us, but can actually prevent us from recognizing the possibilities for love that exist all around us.

The universal Law of Attraction states that we draw to us those people, events, and circumstances that match our inner state of being. In other words, we attract experiences that are consistent with our beliefs. If we believe that there is plenty of love in the world and we are worthy of giving and receiving that love, we will attract a different quality of relationships than someone who believes in scarcity or feels unworthy of happiness. If we believe the world is a loving and friendly place, then most of the time that will be our experience. If we believe the world is a chaotic, stressful, and fearful place, then eventually that will become our reality. So, believing and knowing that your soulmate is out there is a critical first step in the formula for manifesting him or her into your life.

If you do not yet believe with 100 percent certainty that your soulmate is out there, you must begin to look for evidence that will make a believer out of you. When deep down in the core of your being you believe that your soulmate exists, there is no limit to the ways he or she can enter your life. Take for example my friend Trudy, who, while searching for the perfect cantaloupe, met her husband in the produce aisle of a Whole Foods market. Or Patricia, a former colleague, whose best friend practically had to drag her out of bed to go to a party, where she ended up meeting her future husband by the coat check. What about the experience of Gayle Seminara-Mandel, whose story you'll read in a subsequent chapter? Sporting a post-facial blotchy face and sweatpants, she ended up working out next to her future husband on the exercise bikes at the gym where she found herself on a dateless New Year's Eve. Sean Roach, whose story you will also read, was flying back from a three-week trip to Australia, wondering if he would ever find the right woman to marry and start a family with. After an argument erupted in the aisle, he stood up to defend the flight attendant from the harsh words of a rude passenger and found himself gazing into the eyes of his future wife. Do you think Englishman David Brown had any way of knowing he would one day wake up with a cell-phone number running through his head, send a text message to it, and end up striking up a friendship with the owner of the phone that would ultimately blossom into love?

The point is, it is not necessary for you to know how or where or when your soulmate will appear. Your only work right now is to begin to nurture the belief that he or she exists and that you will find each other when the time is right.

You also need to begin to dismantle some of the negative beliefs about yourself that you may have unknowingly collected over the years. For example, deep down inside, do you believe you are loveable? If you are reading this, then I am certain you are lovable. Why? Because lovable people always want more love in their lives. But if you believe you are not lovable, you must start to challenge that belief. I know many very attractive, successful, single people who have some very negative, limiting beliefs when it comes to finding their soulmates. Their list usually goes something like this:

I'm too old.

I'm too fat.

I'm too damaged.

I have too much baggage.

I'm not successful enough.

I'm too successful.

All the good ones are taken.

Nobody I am interested in would be interested in me.

These are just knee-jerk excuses that keep us stuck. There is plenty of evidence that love is available to everyone regardless of age, weight, income, or any of the other factors that we believe limit us. Regardless of our personal histories in relationships, we can choose to adopt the belief that everything we've been through has been but preparation for finding our true love.

My friend Linda Sivertsen, after grieving the end of her nineteen-year marriage at the age of forty-three, is living proof that believing the love you desire exists is the first essential step to drawing it into your life.

Linda's Story
The Second-Chances Prophetic Treasure Map

It was springtime, and things had never seemed better between my husband and me. Was it the beautiful weather or the passing of time that was mellowing my blustery alpha male? He no longer seemed so easily angered or quick to find fault with me. He no longer yelled or called me names or threatened to leave at the smallest disagreement—well, not that often anyway. I've read that increases in estrogen and decreases in testosterone have a calming effect on men as they get older. Thank you, middle age. If harmony is what you bring, I'm happy to trade in the roller-coaster highs and lows for a few wrinkles.

Still, deep down I was sad I had gone my entire adult life longing to know what it would be like living in a partnership without emotional walls or eggshells to walk on. I had longed to stand before my beloved, our pure, open hearts holding space for one another. But I had concluded that this vulnerable kind of love just wasn't in the cards for me, reasoning that this is what you get when you marry a stranger, as I had, after only eight weeks of dating. Could I really have expected an easy road? But then again, is life easy for anyone?

Despite too many hard times to count, we had built a good life. He called me his best friend, and we laughed a lot, had many things in common, and adored our son, which made our lack of passion easier to get my head around. Our views on parenting were vastly different and a source of great pain for us both, but our son was almost off to college, and we'd finally have the time and money to travel and get to know each other outside of the stress of parenting. Although I had doubts about our potential, maybe with his sudden peacefulness, new levels of closeness and intimacy were possible? Maybe there was a way we could open up to the kind of love I hoped in my heart was possible between two people committed to each other?

But three days before our nineteenth anniversary, I discovered the source of my husband's joy—he was having an affair with a woman in another state with two young children who "needed" him and made him feel alive. Their bond was all he needed to walk away from me, from us, and soon move twelve hundred miles away. In an instant, my plans, my dreams, our potential were gone. As he ran toward his bright, shiny future, I was left in the fetal position, grieving the loss of my family (and possibly my home) and trying to deliver on the biggest work deadlines of my life while getting almost no sleep for months on end. The scariest part? Trying to hold up our teenage son, who felt that a nuke had just been detonated in our living room.

Grieving became my daily practice. Losing both of my parents in the previous decade had taught me how to do that. Neighbors saw me walking my dogs, tears streaming down my face. I knew that time would only exaggerate the pain if I didn't get all the dark, lumpy, crappy bits from my heart and mind up and out. I'd scream into pillows and cry so hard I could barely find the energy to drag myself up off the ground. I knew if I didn't purge this man, his betrayal, and our lost life from every possible fiber of my being, I'd be left emotionally handicapped—with a fraction of my self-esteem—wholly in danger of being forever jaded toward men, love, and the very institution of marriage I so believed in.

But within four or five months, I knew something else to be true as well. My ex had freed me. He had done me a favor because there *was* BIG LOVE for me out there—the kind I had always hoped could happen for me. I could feel it, and I started thanking God for the woman who had taken my ex's affections so I could be free. My sister joked that we should send her flowers because the peace I was starting to feel all by myself was beyond the joy I had ever felt being married.

Despite the fact that I was starting to very much enjoy the quiet of being alone, I could feel that "he," my soulmate, was close by and would be a welcome complement to the happiness I was already feeling. I knew he would fulfill needs within me that were never met in my marriage (as, I'm sure, my ex-husband's girlfriend fulfilled for him). "I feel someone very special coming," I told my therapist, "but I'm not ready. I know I need a lot of time to heal." "Linda," she answered. "You have so much love to give. My sense is that you've been ready for a long time. Maybe even years." When friends told me I shouldn't date seriously for a year, my therapist's words helped bolster my inner knowing. I didn't care what anyone said. I was in no mood to lose many months or years keeping myself safe because of someone else's idea of how I should recover from this loss. If BIG LOVE was on its way, I wasn't going to let anything stop Mr. Big from entering my world. I would clean up my life and make the space for him to curl up in the lap of what I knew I still had left to give.

I joined a gym. I started going out with my girlfriends. I put myself out there. I began dating casually. A lot. I wasn't remotely ready to be physically intimate with anyone, other than a few kisses, and I didn't bring anyone home to meet my son. It was mostly light and easy, breezy friendships with men who were helping me remember how to flirt and open myself up. But beneath the casualness and sometimes seeming ridiculous futility of it all (after all, I was out there dating—*hello*?!), I was looking for my partner with full intention. I would imagine him standing behind me, holding me in his arms and kissing the back of my neck. I could feel him as if he were in the flesh. Each day, he was getting closer and closer—I had no doubt—which made it somewhat hard not being obsessed with how I would recognize him when he arrived. So I decided to be proactive.

The next day, my dear friend Arielle Ford and her husband, Brian (both had been on "Team Linda" after my separation, sending me uplifting music and calling regularly with their cheerleading), sent me the Soulmate Kit, with details about how to make the most powerful Treasure Map for attracting one's soulmate. I couldn't wait to get started, to further clarify the image of what having him in my life would look like.

Years ago I had made several such maps, one for a home I'd hoped to manifest (which happened, with remarkable like-ness) and one for my writing career (also with striking results). In fact, I went a little nuts back then with the scissors and had cut out so many extra words and images that I'd put hundreds of them in a box ready for another time. I had to find that box! Sure enough, it was tucked away in the back of a closet.

I painted a red canvas and spent hours going through maga-zines and searching through my previous cutouts for the perfect

> A soulmate is someone to whom
> we feel profoundly connected,
> as though the communication
> and communing that take
> place between us were not the
> product of intentional efforts,
> but rather a divine grace.
> This kind of relationship is so
> important to the soul that many
> have said there is nothing more
> precious in life.
>
> *Thomas Moore*

ones. I would make this map a work of art—simple and beautiful—and include only those words and images that conjured the feelings I wanted to create—words like "bliss," "authentic," "responsible," "man at his best," "easy on the eyes," "best place in the Universe" (referring to four bare feet sticking out of the covers at the end of a bed), and "great minds think alike."

Then I found something strange while going through the box: a large cutout of a name—CHRIS—in white writing on a blue background. That was odd. How did that name get there? I was sure I'd never cut out a name other than my own or my husband's before. Hmmm. This was crazy to me, because I had just had an amazing date with a man named Chris the previous week. But he was so busy transitioning into a different aspect of his work, and we hadn't connected about another date yet. I'd been hoping he would call but was regretfully becoming resigned to the fact that he might not. Could this be a sign? God, I hoped so. I was definitely more attracted to him than any of the other men I'd dated (or, truthfully, anyone I'd met or seen out in the world during my nineteen years of marriage).

The fact that I had cut out Chris's name several years before nagged at me for a few hours. It wasn't small either—much larger than most all the other cutouts. (I'd also been wearing a Saint Christopher medal around my neck for the past year—something I bought myself as a gift before my husband left—which made the CHRIS cutout seem all that much more auspicious.) Finally, the only explanation I could come up with was that I had probably seen the word "CHRISTMAS" in a magazine at one time and cut it out for my best friend, Diane, who's married to a Chris, in case I ever made her a Treasure Map. The only thing was, I had never made her one, had never planned to make her one, and doubted I ever would.

I worked on my soulmate Treasure Map in my kitchen for several days, perfecting it until it felt totally "cooked." One Tuesday afternoon, I carried it upstairs to my bedroom, nailed a nail into the wall, and hung my creation across from my bed. I said a little prayer that it would bring my ideal man into my world, touching each image on the map and then letting it go, trying to trust in my map's inherent magic.

That same evening, Chris called and said he had a headache from a very stressful day at work and was just going to get in the car and go for a ride. "Why don't you drive out to my house?" I said, without any concern that it was already late, that I lived forty minutes away, or about the "rules" women banter about for insisting men call ahead of time for a proper date. *"Forget rules!"* I thought. *"I'm forty-three years old and aching to see this guy.*

Chris came over, I fed him leftovers, and we hit it off so thoroughly that evening that we've been practically inseparable ever since. My handsome man and I are now very much in love. My divorce is weeks away from being final, and he and I talk frequently about sharing our lives together. When he saw my Treasure Map for the first time, he seemed sort of mesmerized by it, scanning the images. A few weeks later, while he was again looking at the map, I was a little nervous but shared the story about his name being in the box. "Why don't you put it on the board?" he said. "Really? Are you sure? Because that's a big step," I said, laughing. The next day, I showed him the cutout of his name and said, "Where do you want me to put it?" He looked at my Treasure Map and told me to paste it in the section I had created on marriage. I looked at him to see if he was teasing, but he just smiled and told me again to paste it there. So I did. Happily.

Time will tell if Chris and I will indeed get married and end up together for the rest of our lives. I can't imagine that not being the case. He's everything I asked for on the map, and then some. But all sappiness aside, the way I see it, being together forever is not really the point. After all, I married my husband, thinking we would be life partners, as in *always together until death do us part (or longer)*, but life is long, and people change and evolve. Regardless, the fun, passion, and gentleness that Chris has already brought into my life feel so deep and profoundly healing that it's as if he has helped wash away a world of pain. And his love has helped me feel safe enough to establish good communications with my ex, both for the sake of our son and to honor the good we did share over so many years.

Like the images and words outlined on my map, Chris looks at me in a way that makes me feel loved, adored, admired, and deeply desired. And in giving him that same love and admiration, I am feeling whole and in partnership in a way I've never known. Now when I'm working in the kitchen or brushing my teeth, he often walks up behind me, wraps me in his arms, and kisses the back of my neck. For me, it just doesn't get any better than that.

• • •

Following the devastating breakup of her marriage, Linda could have allowed her life to be governed by her old belief that "finding real love is not in the cards for me." Instead, she chose to believe that "bad" things happen for good reasons—usually to clear out space for the good that is on its way. I designed the following feelingization to support you in releasing old, limiting beliefs about yourself, others, and the world, that may be preventing you from attracting the love you desire. Remember, you can read this to yourself or download it at http://www .soulmatesecret.com/audio and listen to it with your eyes closed.

Feelingization
Releasing Old Beliefs

Begin by taking a moment to remember your worst romantic encounters—the people who really weren't kind and loving; the ones you'd like to forget; the ones who hurt you the most, who betrayed your trust, who caused your heart to shut down.

Now imagine these past lovers are all standing in front of you. Allow yourself to feel the pain they caused you in the past.

Take a moment to ask yourself what you must have believed about yourself to tolerate this kind of behavior. Did you believe you didn't deserve any better? That you had no right to ask for more? That you weren't lovable?

Now, take a deep breath and ask yourself, "Am I willing to release these old beliefs?" Notice what your answer is, and if you are really ready to let them go, imagine gathering all the old, painful feelings and beliefs and limitations and mentally projecting them onto all your old lovers, who are still standing before you. Just imagine dumping all those old painful feelings back onto those ex-lovers. Take a moment to notice how that feels.

Now imagine you have an aerosol can—like a spray-paint can—in your hand. See yourself pointing it at those ex-lovers. In a moment, you're going to press the trigger and spray the can, and as you do, all those people and all those painful memories are going to become globbed together inside a big latex bubble.

Take a moment and relish the feeling of spraying that paint, congealing every one of those negative memories, experiences, and beliefs together into a single bubble. They are now separate from you, removed from you. Take a deep breath and enjoy the freedom of that.

Now imagine that in your left hand you are holding a large, sharp needle. Perhaps a smile comes across your face just imagining what I'm about to ask you to do. That's right, when you are ready, take the needle and puncture that latex bubble, watching it explode and disappear into thin air.

These people are now gone from your consciousness . . . and with them the painful feelings, beliefs, and experiences of the past. Feel what it feels like to no longer carry the burden of your past with you. Feel the freedom, the new possibilities, the relief.

Take a deep breath, and notice what arises when I ask you this question:

What would you have to believe about yourself in order to magnetize your soulmate into your life?

Would you have to believe and know you are lovable? That you are deserving? That you are a fabulous catch?

Believe and know deep in your heart that The One is out there for you, that you deserve to have your desires fulfilled, and that you deserve to give and receive love.

And if you don't quite believe it today, see if you can, in this moment, believe that The One is on the way and that your knowingness is growing daily.

• • •

Take this time to think about all the qualities you have to offer, and in case you are forgetting what those are, I'd like to remind you: it's the love you give and share, the kindness and warmth you exude—not to mention all your other talents.

> You were born to be loved, cherished, and adored.
> You were born to be loved, cherished, and adored.
> You were born to be loved, cherished, and adored.

Repeat this to yourself seven times, allowing it to penetrate deeply into your heart.

Ultimately, it's not your job to know *HOW* your soulmate is going to appear. It's only your job to be ready, willing, and open to receive your soulmate's love. You don't exactly know where air or water come from, but you totally believe they are there for you. As a human being, you know that air and water are part of your divine inheritance. No matter what mistakes you have made in the past, you are still going to wake up every day and have access to air and water. The same is true for love. It's there for you. It's always been there for you. You just need to remember the love that you are, and once you do, the Universe will bring you more of it. In other words, there is nothing for you to do; there is only a way for you to *be*. Be the loving person you are; live in the knowingness that you deserve to have a loving, committed relationship; and savor the waiting for your beloved to arrive.

Believing that your soulmate exists, that you are deserving of him or her, and that the Universe is skillfully orchestrating your meeting is the basis for applying the next part of the formula—to generate a vision of yourself and your life where these beliefs are your daily reality.

TREASURE MAPPING FOR LOVE

Treasure mapping is a powerful tool for manifestation, because it helps you to both intuitively and objectively clarify what your heart is yearning to experience. A Treasure Map acts as a visual reminder of the life you are committed to creating. I have been making Treasure Maps for years, and it's uncanny how many of the images and ideas that I mapped have manifested in my actual life. Once, after Brian and I had just found out we would need to move within nine months, I made a Treasure Map that included a picture of a bedroom with an ocean view we found particularly appealing. When it was time to go house hunting, the very first home we saw had a master bedroom with this same view, the same carpet, and the same wooden frame around the windows. It was exactly what we had imagined. This is the power of Treasure Mapping.

You can make your Treasure Map 100 percent focused on attracting your soulmate, or you can separate it into four life areas:

1 love & relationship

2 health & fitness

3 career & money

4 spiritual & emotional fulfillment

To create your Treasure Map, you will need:

❐ a good-sized piece of poster board or foam board

❐ a stack of your favorite magazines that reflect your
unique interests and taste

❐ a glue stick and a pair of scissors

❐ several hours to devote to this project

Flip through the magazines and cut out images, words, and photographs that appeal to you. Try not to think too hard about the words and images you're selecting, but rather trust your gut feeling about what you find attractive. Make sure to include at least one photo or image of a loving couple—it could be as simple as two people walking on the beach hand in hand. When selecting these images, you are looking to evoke a feeling as opposed to manifesting the models in the photos, so look for images that convey the feeling you desire more than a particular face. Images that represent love, romance, commitment, and joy are all good. If marrying your soulmate is what you desire, feel free to add engagement rings, wedding rings, wedding cakes, or anything else that is a symbol of marriage or commitment. You should also include a photo of yourself looking really happy, and surround that image with words that express your positive beliefs about finding love. You want your Treasure Map to affirm that you are loved, cherished, and adored by your perfect partner.

I have heard about so many incredible connections unfolding as a result of people using the Treasure Mapping process. On the surface it seems unbelievable or miraculous, but I now understand that Treasure Mapping just helps to reveal attributes that are important to you in a partner, which you may not be consciously aware of. Looking at your map daily reminds you of your deeper values and also helps you to begin noticing them where you may have missed them before. Consider the success my friend Ken Foster had with this process.

Ken's Story
Creating a Map of Love

Many years ago I was in a relationship that looked good from a distance. All our friends thought we were perfect together, but in truth our relationship felt lonely and painful. Rather than supporting one another's growth, we seemed to feed off each other's weaknesses, and we experienced major dramas almost daily. I knew I deserved to have a great relationship—one that nurtured my soul and enlivened my spirit—but for the moment I was feeling stuck and depressed. I wanted out, but I didn't want to run from another bad relationship. I wanted to move toward a great one.

It was during this time that I began working with a teacher who assured me I could have whatever I wanted in life if I learned to use the power of my mind. This teacher suggested that if I wanted to have a great relationship, I would have to change some of my core beliefs about how the Universe works. She told me that whatever I was picturing on the inside of my mind was going to show up on the outside, because of something called the Law of Attraction. My assignment was to get clear about the exact kind of relationship I wanted and then have faith that it would actually show up for me. I was a little skeptical, but I was also ready for a change, so I decided to give it a try.

I put together a dream board that would serve as a visual reminder of what I wanted to manifest in my life—and of course I was looking to manifest the woman who would one day be my wife. While flipping through a magazine, I was struck by a picture of a brunette relaxing in a tropical setting, her head tilted back, and aqua blue water flowing over her head. Her eyes were partially open, and in her slight smile I could detect a look of ecstasy. Gazing at this picture, I felt I was getting a sneak peek at my actual soulmate. I knew she would be beautiful, deeply spiritual, healthy, nurturing, kindhearted, loving, and loyal.

As a result of creating my dream board, I became very clear about what the nonnegotiable characteristics and behaviors of my next partner would be. But I still wasn't clear about what I needed to embrace inside of me for my soulmate to appear. One day while I was meditating on my dream board, I heard a small, quiet voice inside of me say, *"Live with certainty."* At first I didn't know what that meant, but then I started to understand. I had been living my life with so much doubt—I doubted I would attract the right partner; I doubted my abilities to be a good provider; I doubted my spiritual path; I doubted I could remain married; I doubted that the dream board would work. I had so many doubts, and one day it dawned on me that this was exactly the reason I was stuck. The woman I was meant to attract was no match for the doubts I had allowed to run rampant in my mind.

In that instant I resolved to stop living my life from a place of doubt. I consciously and deliberately renewed my faith in every way I could: I focused on my strengths, and to the best of my ability, I lived from a place of certainty, trusting and following the impulses I received from within.

Within one week of making that decision, Judy became visible to me. I say she became visible because we had actually met several years earlier—at the Shared Vision luncheon my teacher took me to! Over the years we had become friends, but my eyes were so clouded with doubt and uncertainty that I could not see who she really was.

I asked Judy to marry me after we had dated for just a month. We spent our honeymoon on Kauai, and one day as we were swimming together in a tropical pool, I noticed a special rock formation where the aquamarine water was flowing through. I asked Judy to lean back under the waterfall so I could take a picture, and I caught a glimpse of the magic of the Universe. When we got the pictures back, I was speechless. The picture I took that day was the exact picture from my dream board: the brunette in the bathing suit with long hair, being caressed by a waterfall, with the look of ecstasy that had so captivated me. Only this time she wasn't a dream; she was my wife. Today we live what most would consider a dream life in San Diego, California. We have been married for nine years, and it keeps getting better and better.

• • •

Once you've created your Treasure Map, I would suggest you keep it in a place where you can look at it daily but slide it under the bed or in a closet when company shows up. You don't need anyone else's opinions or energy projected onto your dreams and commitments. Your Treasure Map is just for you. I like to set up my Treasure Map as an altar with candles, fresh flowers, and spiritual icons nearby to bless it. You can also place it in the relationship corner of your bedroom (more about this in chapter 3) as a reminder of all you have to offer and all you are ready to receive.

Remember, what you believe to be true about yourself in the innermost recesses of your heart and mind is what gets mirrored back to you through your external circumstances. This is incredibly good news! Because while you may have justified the belief that you are only talented enough to attract a certain amount of money or only organized enough to accomplish a certain number of daily tasks, there is virtually no limit or worldly barometer that can measure your inner worth. You are inherently lovable, and the moment you start believing that with all your heart and mind, you will begin to see evidence of it all around you. Now is the time to see yourself as you want your beloved to see you and to treat yourself as you would have him or her treat you. You wouldn't long to find true love unless you were capable of being such a lover.

CHAPTER TWO

readiness

...

I have found that if you love life,
life will love you back.

Arthur Rubinstein

In the process of becoming ready to manifest my soulmate, I met with Jeremiah Abrams, a Jungian psychotherapist and the founder of Mount Vision Institute in California. Jeremiah gently guided me to see aspects of myself that I hadn't been willing to admit before—including the defenses I was unconsciously using to keep love away. One of the most valuable ways he supported me in getting ready to meet my soulmate was by simply holding the space for my perfect relationship to unfold. He said, both verbally and nonverbally, "I so believe in your dream of finding your soulmate that I am going to make it my dream as well." Together we held the vision of me becoming ready on all levels to meet my soulmate, and all the work we did was geared toward this end result. There is tremendous power in making a clear declaration that you are willing to ready yourself on all levels for attracting your life partner.

Think about the idea of readiness in practical terms. If you had a goal to move to a new city, it would likely take you months or even years of preparation before you were actually ready to make the move. You'd have to envision where you wanted to work and live and what kind of lifestyle you'd like to create. You'd probably want to clean out your drawers, your closets, and your files so you could begin your new life with a clean slate. The same principles apply when readying yourself to meet your soulmate—it's imperative that you create emotional, physical, and psychological space in your life and that you actively plan for his or her impending arrival. Nature abhors a vacuum. This means that the faster and more completely we clear out the old, the more rapidly and easily we'll draw in the new.

Just as a gardener prepares the soil before planting new seeds, we must weed the garden of our hearts, bodies, and minds before we'll be ready to receive new love. Although you may insist you are ready—and even that you've been ready for years—I want to suggest that there may still be areas of your life where you're actually blocking, deflecting, or resisting the very thing you desire the most. The purpose of this chapter is to help you identify those places so you can gently but progressively clean them up in preparation for meeting your beloved. As you ask yourself the following questions, I encourage you to reflect on them honestly and take the required actions as you move forward.

1. Is there someone I am still in love with?

If you answered yes to this question, think about this: if you know this person is not your soulmate, and/or there is no possibility of a true, loving, committed relationship with him, would you be willing to give yourself all the time it takes to let him go? I don't believe that you have to stop loving him, but I do believe you need to find a new place in your heart for the love you shared together. When I envision my own heart, I see it as a vast, loving, elastic, sacred space that fits within my chest and expands to encompass everything in the Universe. There is a place in my heart for people I love and am currently in relationship with, and there is a place in my heart for those I have loved but am no longer invested in or directing my attention toward.

There is a place in your heart, too, where you can still love those who were once in your life without wasting any of your precious time wanting them again. So often people will tell you to "just forget about them" when, really, that just isn't possible. I think a lot of pain comes from resisting our true feelings for those we once loved. Instead, allow yourself to love them, but do not allow yourself to be consumed by thoughts of being with them.

As thoughts of a former love come up, acknowledge them and then gently tuck them into your special heart chamber, then turn your attention back to the present moment. If you find yourself obsessing, wishing, hoping, or fantasizing about what you can't have (or what isn't in your highest and best good), it then becomes an issue of managing your emotions. Many great forms of therapy and emotional processes can help you with this, including Eye Movement Desensitization and Reprocessing (EMDR), hypnosis, and the Sedona Method, which supports people in letting go of loss and pain. Be willing to spend the time and money to get professional support if you need it. I certainly did my share of therapy and workshops and found all of it incredibly useful. It doesn't matter if you've been working on the same issue for the past twenty years. Know that every time you move through some issue that has kept your heart closed, you liberate suppressed energy and free up valuable space in your life.

2. *Is there someone I am still angry with, feel betrayed by, or haven't forgiven?*

You may not realize it, but resenting someone binds you just as tightly to that person as longing does. Both are attachments that keep you hooked in the past rather than focused clearly in the present moment. Before we can accept new love into our lives, we have to release any hurt and upset we're still holding on to from the past. The following exercise will provide a lot of relief.

What you will need:

❏ several sheets of paper and a pen

❏ comfortable chair

❏ fifteen to thirty minutes of uninterrupted time

To begin, make a list of the ex-lovers with whom you feel incomplete or toward whom you are still harboring grudges or resentments.

Write a letter to each of them that expresses, in detail, all the things you are still angry about and wish had turned out differently. You will most likely never mail these letters, so give yourself permission to go full out. See if you can identify what you need—from them or from yourself—in order to find resolution with each situation. Once you have completed this step, you should be feeling calm enough to also acknowledge the role you played in the breakdown of your relationships and to apologize for anything you've done that you regret.

> For one human being to love another; that is perhaps the most difficult of all our tasks, the ultimate, the last test and proof, the work for which all other work is but preparation.
>
> *Rainer Maria Rilke*

Once you have written your letter to each ex-lover, write a second letter for each—this time from your ex-loves to you, *from their perspectives*. Doing this is not as difficult as it sounds: Choose a place in your house where they once sat (if possible); then, as you imagine them sitting in front of you, move your body so you are now sitting where they sat, seeing what they saw, and feeling what they must have felt. Imagine your ex-lovers moving the pen over the paper as each shares the version of his or her relationship with you. After you've written these letters, read them out loud to yourself with the intention of allowing any remaining animosity or resentment to move through you.

You'll have an opportunity to go deeper into the process of unhooking from the past in chapter 6, but this exercise in and of itself should leave you feeling a bit more lightness and space in your heart.

3. Is there room in my life for another person?

Be honest: do you really have the time and energy right now to devote to a deep, loving, committed relationship? If you don't have time now, when will you? If you don't get an answer, try this little exercise: Close your eyes for a minute, and imagine you are sitting in a movie theater facing a large, black screen. As you are sitting in this dark theater ask your wiser self to project onto the screen in big red letters the month and year you will be ready. If you got an answer, great. If you didn't, I encourage you to spend some time looking deeper into the matter to see what relationships, commitments, or projects you'll need to attend to before you will feel ready. You might discover, like my friend Marci Shimoff did, that there are some big, important projects that you are meant to complete before you will be truly ready to manifest your soulmate.

Marci's Story
He's Your Destiny

As far back as I can remember, I always dreamed of being with my soulmate. It wasn't so much the fairy tale version of Prince Charming I was looking for but rather a deep connection with the man I felt was part of my life's destiny, a man my soul would recognize as home.

From the time I was nine years old, I would lie in bed at night asking God where my soulmate was. I would always get the same answer: Italy. Now that was a strange answer for a young girl growing up in California to hear. But somehow it felt right. Along with that answer, I would see a face. I couldn't make out all the details, but he had dark hair and a moustache and was dashingly handsome.

By the age of twenty-two, I was starting to feel discouraged that I hadn't met "him" yet. About that time, I took a seminar on success in which I was taught that my goals should be clear and specific and that I should write them down. Thus began a series of "soulmate wish lists." I wrote down every quality I was looking for in a man. Each time I'd make the list, I'd manage to come up with sixty to seventy qualities, with "spiritual" and "powerful" at the top. Those two would always vie for first place, "spiritual" winning out when I was in a meditative mood a "powerful" edging out a victory when I was on a career roll. I'd slip each new list into the file folder I labeled Soulmate. I still have that folder—complete with the twenty-three lists I compiled over the years.

During those years, I had five significant relationships with wonderful men. But there was one consistent problem: with each, I had the nagging feeling that he wasn't The One. We'd break up because I wanted to make room for Mr. Soulmate. In retrospect, I wish I had just enjoyed being with them for the time we were together and trusted that "he" would come along at the right time.

The rest of my life was going splendidly. I had a fabulous career: I had coauthored *Chicken Soup for the Woman's Soul* and *Chicken Soup for the Mother's Soul*, books that had become No. 1 New York Times bestsellers, selling millions of copies. I was traveling around the world, giving speeches and seminars to thousands of people. I was at the top of my career game. But life on the road felt empty, and I was really longing for "him."

I spent a lot of time wondering why others found their soulmates but I couldn't find mine. What was I doing wrong? Why was God punishing me? I'd torment myself with these questions and beat myself up for not being able to find him. Whenever I'd complain to my mother, she would comfort me by saying, "Don't worry, honey. He'll be worth the wait."

Then my business partner, Jennifer Hawthorne, and I came up with an idea for a new Chicken Soup for the Soul book—for singles who, like me, wanted to hear stories about being single *and* happy. That was the premise of the book: you don't need a partner to be happy. We began writing that book in 1998, just after my fortieth birthday. During the year I spent working on the book, I let go of my need for a soulmate and shifted my attention to being happy inside.

A deep knowingness came over me. I had a sense that as soon as the book was published, my "single karma" would be over. In fact, I used to say to Jennifer almost daily: "When this book is done, I'm done being single." I said it, I felt it, I believed it—but amazingly, without any attachment about how or when it would happen. Meanwhile, I went about creating my own happiness.

Then one cold Iowa day in January 1999, I had a most unusual meeting. I trudged through slushy piles of snow to a nondescript building where a little Indian man was sitting in a conference room, waiting to give me a reading from palm leaves. According to his tradition, a person's destiny is written in Sanskrit on these ancient dried palm-leaf scrolls. He flipped through a tall stack of leaves until he landed on my scroll. He knew absolutely nothing about me, except my name and birth time and place, but he proceeded to tell me all about myself and my future.

His first words were, "You have a great life," to which I agreed. Then he said, "But let's talk about the no-husband problem."

He told me that over the next six months, I would meet three eligible men, one right after the other. All of them would be foreign-born, and while I'd have a nice connection with each of them, they would become just good friends. I told him his prediction was impossible—I never met eligible men one right after the other. There were always a few years in between my relationships, so the scenario he painted seemed ridiculous to me. He insisted it would happen and went on to reveal the news I had come to hear.

"Then you'll meet a fourth man—he's your husband. Let me describe him to you, so you'll know him. He'll have dark hair and a moustache and look Mediterranean. He was born and raised in Italy. He'll be working with people as a therapist, helping them with their life problems. He'll love music, dance, and the arts. He'll be living in California. And," he went on, "he'll be six years younger than you."

"Impossible!" I blurted out again, this time not hiding my frustration. "I *never* date younger men. Every man I've ever dated has been older than me, usually about ten years older. I don't even *like* younger men."

He said, "I can't help it. He's your destiny."

I left the meeting thinking this Indian man was very sweet but off his rocker. I dismissed the whole thing and went about my life, forgetting about a soulmate and putting my attention back on making my own happiness.

Strangely enough, two weeks later, I started dating a European man. About a month after that, I went out with another man, who was from England, and we became good friends.

About two months later, I was set up on a blind date with yet another man—this one from Russia. We, too, became great friends. I know it's hard to believe, but throughout this time, I didn't remember the palm-leaf reading. I had dismissed it so completely that it never once crossed my mind that the first part of his prediction had already come true.

On September 15, 1999, *Chicken Soup for the Single's Soul* was released in bookstores. The very next day, I went to the Omega Institute, a beautiful retreat center in the Catskill Mountains of New York, to attend a personal-growth course with more than six hundred people. After pulling into the large gravel parking lot and finding a parking space, I got out of my car, and the first person I saw was Karen, a woman I had become friends with the previous year at another course I'd taken at Omega. I thought this was an amazing synchronicity, as she was the only person I'd befriended at the event the prior year. She was just about to get into her car to leave, as the course she'd attended had finished.

After hugging each other hello, she said out of the blue, "Do you want to meet a man?" I replied, "I always want to meet a man."

She then told me about a man she'd met at the dance course she'd just attended. She thought I'd like him. He was staying on to take the course I'd come for, and she wanted to introduce us.

She asked, "Do you like big, macholike men?"

"Yes!" I answered, enthusiastically.

"Well, he's not that," she said. "He's more the soft, sensitive type."

"Hmmm, not what I had in mind . . .," I thought.

Then she asked, "Do you like older men?"

"Oh, yeah!" I said with excitement.

"Well, he's not that either," she said. "I think he's probably five or six years younger than you."

Completely deflated, I said, "In that case, no; I really don't want to meet him."

At exactly that moment, she turned and out of the corner of her eye saw him walking across the other side of the parking lot and pointed at him. He was so far away that I couldn't see his face, but I got a sense of his energy and immediately grabbed her arm and said, "I've got to meet him." We rushed across the parking lot.

Karen said, "Sergio, I want you to meet my friend Marci. You must teach her to dance." Before I could even say hello, Sergio took me in his arms and waltzed me around the gravel parking lot. I'd just been introduced to my Italian Prince Charming.

We felt an instant rapport, as though we'd known each other forever. But we certainly didn't fit each other's soulmate picture. Temperamentally, we were so different. He was easygoing, mellow, and laid back. I was energetic, enthusiastic, and a "handful." We had a very challenging first few months, trying to maintain a long-distance relationship (I'd travel from Iowa to California to see him every few weeks), and I wasn't at all sure our disparate personalities could ever get along.

Then one morning just as I was waking up at home in Iowa, I flashed on the session with the palm-leaf reader I'd completely forgotten about. I jumped out of bed and ran to the file that held my notes from that meeting. Going over them, I was blown away. I picked up the phone and called Sergio, waking him at five in the morning to read him the paragraph:

"He'll have dark hair and a moustache and look Mediterranean. He was born and raised in Italy. He'll be working with people as a therapist, helping them with their life problems. He'll love music, dance, and the arts. He'll be living in California. *And* he'll be six years younger than you."

Every point was completely accurate. We were silent for a few moments.

Just then, a memory came floating to the surface in my mind. The face of the man in my childhood dreams—it was Sergio's face, my soulmate.

We've been together for almost a decade. The Indian palm-leaf reader was right: Sergio is my destiny. And my mother was right: he was worth the wait!

• • •

Marci's introduction to Sergio would not have happened as it did had she not committed to putting her affairs in order by finishing her book. Readiness means just that—preparing

ourselves on all levels so that when our soulmates unexpectedly enter our lives and waltz us across a gravel parking lot, we
are ready for the dance.

4. Am I physically ready?

During my days as a book publicist, one of my first respon-
sibilities with new clients was to give them advice on how to
present themselves during television appearances. First im-
pressions do count, and your hair and clothing should show
you off at your best. I once met with a potential client—a forty-
five-year-old Ph.D.—who looked like she wanted to be a sev-
enteen-year-old cheerleader. Her overbleached, long blond
hair, short skirt, and pink lipstick were in complete contrast
to her resume. I tried to explain that it would be nearly impossible to take her seriously, because her look did not match the
level of professionalism she claimed to possess. As gently as
possible, I explained the importance of looking the part, but
in the end this woman was more committed to her miniskirts
than to advancing her career.

If your dream man or woman is an important corporate ex-
ecutive and you're sporting purple streaks in your hair and
avant-garde clothes, you may be adding unnecessary road-
blocks to your love life. In addition to clothing style, the colors we wear have the power to influence our emotions, our
energy, and the way others view us. A red power suit on a woman

is great in a corporate setting but probably a bit over the top when attending a social event. Begin to think about what you're communicating with the colors, textures, and styles of your clothes. Like it or not, we size up one another pretty quickly based on appearances. Use this information to your benefit, and be deliberate about the nonverbal messages you're sending. Now would be a great time to explore the possibility of updating your image and wardrobe. If you haven't changed your hairstyle (or color) in the last five or ten years, consider getting a consultation at the hottest hair salon in town to explore your options.

The bottom line is this: When we look good, we feel good. When we feel good about ourselves, it radiates, and we are more confident. Preparing to manifest your soulmate is a perfect time to nurture your most beautiful self.

The following feelingization will support you in creating space in your heart and life for new love.

Feelingization
Clearing the Space for Love

Find a comfortable seat, engage your imagination, and in your mind's eye visualize the driveway in front of your house. If you live in a tall condo with no driveway, pick the house you grew up in, or pick any house that you have ever been in that has a driveway, and for the purpose of this exercise, that's your house.

I want you to imagine that your ex—someone with whom you still feel attached in either a positive or a negative way—has parked his car right in the middle of your driveway. If your ex didn't have a car, make up the kind of car you think he would have had. So, you are looking at the car of your ex-lover, sitting parked in your driveway. Maybe you're standing right next to it; maybe you're peering at it from a window or through a crack in the door. Notice any feelings that arise as you view this scene.

As you are looking at the car, you suddenly catch a glimpse of the biggest, baddest tow truck you have ever seen. It looks like one of those monster trucks with wheels that are nearly as tall as a normal car. At first you think it's going to drive right by . . . but then you realize it's pulling right up to your ex's car! It backs up to it, and, sure enough, out comes the tow-truck driver, who lowers that big hook right onto the bumper. Watch as the tow truck raises half the car up off the ground, and listen as the truck engine cranks up. Now the tow truck is driving forward and pulling your ex's car out of your driveway. Notice how that feels.

After the tow truck has pulled away, you look down, and the first thing you notice is that the driveway where your ex's car was parked is filthy. There's grease, oil, and dirt everywhere, and it looks like a mess. You look back to see where the tow truck is taking the car, and you see that it's heading out of your neighborhood. It's now on the highway or the freeway closest to your house and heading north. So, if you are on the East Coast, the tow truck pulling your ex's car is on I-95 headed north toward Canada; if you are on the West Coast, it's on I-5 headed north toward Alaska; if you are in any other part of the country, pick the closest freeway and have it head north toward the North Pole.

The tow truck keeps traveling north, and soon it's just passed the North Pole. It's picking up speed now. It's going faster and faster until finally . . . you notice it has lifted off the ground entirely! It's flying through the air like a plane taking off. You watch it make its way up through the clouds, and then you see the tow-truck driver, who has skillfully parachuted to safety. The tow truck, with your ex's car in tow, is now in outer space and continues to head to the far reaches of the universe. It has just passed out of the Milky Way, and it has already passed several black holes. You are not in the tow truck, by the way; you are at your house, but you can see that the tow truck and the car are now beyond the farthest, farthest reaches of the universe. You suddenly feel something in the palm of your hand, so you look down and see that there is a little box with a *big* red button on it. When I say Go, you are going to push this button and blow the car into a million pieces. Are you ready?

1, 2, 3, go!

The car and the tow truck have just been blown into ten gazillion pieces. You can't even see them because they are so small and so many lightyears away. With a great sense of satisfaction and relief, you turn your attention once again to your driveway, to the spot where your ex's car was parked. Once again, you notice that the driveway has accumulated years and years of abuse, neglect, dirt, and grease. You realize now that this is totally unacceptable, so you gather yourself, roll up your sleeves, and get to work on cleaning the space. On the four corners of the driveway, I want you to imagine yourself placing four very tall candles. These candles can be waist high, or they can be shoulder high, like huge Tiki torches. Make them as high as you would like them to be. You now take a match or a lighter and light the candle at each of the four corners of your driveway.

The moment you light them, you see that a team in hazmat suits is running in. They have cleansers and equipment, and they are starting to clean up the mess on the driveway. The four candles are continuing to burn, and your hazmat crew is taking away the biggest pieces of debris, putting them into their garbage bags. Then they are getting on their truck and going home for the day. Leave the candles burning. They are purifying your space, cleaning out the remnants of the past. These candles are going to burn for the next thirty days, and today is Day One. Take a good look around, because tomorrow at the same time you will come back and continue to clean up your driveway. The moment you put your attention on those four candles burning at the four corners of your driveway, the hazmat team will come with scrub brushes, soap, new paint, asphalt . . . whatever your driveway needs to become fresh and pure and new again. The goal is to make this driveway the most beautiful, gorgeous driveway you have ever seen. Make it very inviting to your soulmate—so he can't wait to pull his car in. Come back each day and see how far down the candles have burned, and see that the grease stains have faded and disappeared, only to be replaced by fresh white pavement and beauty.

Each day as you return, you clean this space up even more, adding plants and flowers around the driveway, and as you do, know that you are rolling out a cosmic welcome mat for your beloved.

• • •

After completing this feelingization, affirm to yourself that you are now ready to welcome new love. The internal space of your body and mind is becoming clear and open. You are making room in your heart for the love of another.

5. Creating soul space

As we've just explored, if you want to be ready, willing, and able to welcome your soulmate into your life, you must carve out the physical, emotional, and mental space that will allow you to recognize his presence and pursue your connection with him. But there is also another kind of space you need to begin to cultivate, and this is the spaciousness that can only arise from quiet reflection and meditation.

I can tell you without a shadow of doubt that most of the people I know who have used the Law of Attraction to find their life partners did not meet them at a crowded party or at a singles function. They met their soulmates when they were silent, still, at peace within themselves, and connected to their deeper wisdom. Readiness is not just about completing projects, updating your image, and saying goodbye to old lovers. It's about generating a degree of stillness inside of you that enables you to feel and hear the faint whispers of intuition that offer you clues to right action.

Having set yourself to the task of making space in your life and becoming ready to welcome your beloved, your only job now is to surrender the timing and allow things to unfold organically. I have come to understand that timing really is everything. To accept this means that we become willing to work on the Universe's timetable rather than clinging stubbornly to our own. Timing and destiny are inevitably entwined and we must learn to trust the divine unfolding of each.

In the book *Eat, Pray, Love* by Elizabeth Gilbert, there is a quote about destiny that I love. She writes:

> Destiny is a play between divine grace and willful self effort. Half of it you have no control over, half of it is absolutely in your hands and your actions will show measurable consequence. Man is neither entirely a puppet of the Gods nor is he entirely the captain of his own destiny. He is a little of both. We gallop through our lives like circus performers balancing on two speeding side-by-side horses. One foot is on the horse called "Faith," the other on the horse called "Free will" and the question you have to ask every day is which horse is which, which horse do I need to stop worrying about because it's not under my control and which do I need to steer with concentrated effort.

In preparing to manifest your soulmate, an element of willful effort and also big elements of faith and destiny are involved. It's a combination of the three that will get you the prize.

CHAPTER THREE

feathering
the nest

...

Ever since happiness heard
your name, it has been running
through the streets trying to find you.

Hanz

Think about the moment when your soulmate first walks through the door of your home. Imagine the sights, sounds, and smells you'd like to greet your lover with as he or she enters your space for the first time. What kind of environment would provide the perfect backdrop for you and this person to fall madly in love? Now, think about your home as it exists in this moment. I am willing to bet there are some areas where an upgrade is in order to get your home ready to welcome in the love of your life.

Remember, the process of manifesting a soulmate is one of making space for her or him on all levels of your being and in all areas of your life. This naturally must include the place where you reside—your home. In this chapter, we'll explore the art of "space clearing" to purge your home of any negative or obstructive energies left over from previous relationships, outdated ideas, or even the influence of previous tenants. Once your home is clean and clear of these obstructions, I'll share some of the Feng Shui secrets I used to transform my home into a magnet for love.

SUBTLE ENERGIES

Our homes are not just shelters made up of four walls, windows, and doors. Ideally, they are havens, inner sanctums that reflect our deepest feelings and highest values. The underlying vibration or feeling you get when you walk into a place is an indication of that home's energy. The sights, smells, and tastes that meet your senses contribute to this feeling, but there is also something more subtle that can only be registered in your gut as a feeling of being comfortable or uncomfortable in a particular environment. When you walk into a room where people have been fighting and feel tension so thick you could cut it with a knife, you are tuning in to the energy of that room. Likewise, when you walk into someone's house and feel instantly at ease, it's often more a function of the energy of the place than any particular architecture or décor.

I have been aware of the subtle energy of things since I was a very young child. I remember lying in our backyard when I was two or three years old, looking at the weeds, which I thought were flowers, and seeing sparkling energy radiating around each one. I also remember walking into different people's homes and being able to feel what kinds of homes they were. There were happy homes, tense homes, angry homes . . . homes that seemed to reach out and welcome me in, and homes that felt like they held many untold secrets. Perhaps you have noticed that different homes emit different vibrations, whether you registered this information consciously or not. Now that you have declared yourself ready to find your soulmate, you need to become extra alert to the energy that your home conveys and take steps to ensure that the message it's sending out is inviting and attractive.

Even if you just moved into a new home or apartment, residual negative energies from your past, the previous occupants, or even the surrounding environment can undermine the mood you are trying to create. Fights you've had there with ex-lovers, times of sadness or grieving, and periods of loneliness or desperation are all retained in your space at an energetic level. In other words, the walls of your home *can* talk, and you want to make sure they are transmitting your readiness for love, passion, commitment, and fulfillment. By clearing your energetic space, you can begin this new, potent period in your life with a fresh clean slate.

As we discussed in the previous chapter, creating space is essential to the process of attracting something new. When making your home ready to receive your soulmate, it's especially important to make room in your bedroom and to keep some space clear in your closet. Along these same lines, I recommend that you keep the nightstand on your soulmate's side of the bed clear and empty so that when this person arrives, he

> "When you walk
> let your heart lead the way
> and you'll find love any day."
>
> *Burt Bacharach*
> (from "Alfie")

or she can fill it with his or her own personal items. Make sure your bed is big enough to sleep two comfortably, and if you are divorced but are sleeping in the bed your ex slept in, it's definitely a good idea to get a new bed—and new sheets.

If you find that you are resistant to letting go of reminders of past loves or making room for your soulmate in your bedroom or your closets, it may be a sign that you are not yet ready to share your life at this level. So if you come across some resistance, use it as an opportunity to do deeper, more emotional work (there are several great exercises in the "Readiness" and "Unhooking the Past" chapters) to overcome any blocks you may still have.

Eliminating physical clutter from your life is one of the fastest ways I know to increase the inflow of new positive energy. Like putting out a "cosmic welcome mat," it sends a clear and specific message to the Universe that you are ready for someone to join your life, feel at home in your environment, and eventually share your bedroom.

Space-clearing rituals are practiced in almost every tradition and native culture in the world. Designed to cleanse and purify the energy, or *chi,* of your home, these techniques remove stagnant energy in your environment and raise the level of consciousness throughout your home. Although there are many space-clearing techniques to choose from, my favorite is a process called smudging.

Native Americans used smudging to cleanse away negative energy with smoke from various herbs or resins, including sage, cedar, sweetgrass, and lavender. The tradition of smudging is becoming more commonplace and is a very simple and pleasant clearing technique. Your local Whole Foods market or metaphysical bookstore will have a variety of products available, including smudge sticks, smudge wands, and smudge bundles. If you prefer, there are professional energy healers and Feng Shui consultants who will come in and do this for you. Select whatever method feels most comfortable to you.

• • •

To begin:

❐ I prefer to use California sage, and I like to smudge during the day. I begin by opening all the doors and windows of my home and letting in as much sunshine and fresh air as possible. I like to begin at the front door and systematically go through the entire house. You want to reach every corner, closet, and room of your entire home. As you do this, be mindful of your intention and your thoughts. In the Native American tradition,

Smudging Ceremony

it is common to pray as you cleanse your home in this way. You can recite one of your favorite prayers or offer up a simple blessing such as this one: "Bless and purify this home and make it a cozy nest for me and my beloved." Remember, your goal is to clear all negative energy from your personal space and to welcome in new, fresh, positive energy that is supportive and loving.

❑ Light the end of the smudge stick and place it either on an abalone shell or in a heatproof dish (you may want to wear an oven mitt on the hand using the smudging herb).

❑ Use your hand or a feather to fan the smoke over the area or object you wish to purify.

If you are cleansing a room, hold the container, and move your hand in large circles as you walk around the room, being mindful of your intention to banish any and all negativity and create space for love to blossom.

Don't forget to move the smoke around all door frames and throughout all closets.

Of course, you should use your best judgment and common sense when smudging with lit objects.

If you don't like the smell of sage, or if you live in a small place or a home with less-than-excellent ventilation, here are some other space-clearing techniques to consider:

✓ *Use* your favorite incense to cleanse and purify your home. Move through each room of your living space with three incense sticks in the manner described above.

✓ *Fill* a glass with clean water, add a bit of your favorite perfume or essential oil, and walk around the house, dabbing the tip of a handkerchief in the glass and then generously spritzing the perfumed water all about with a flick of your wrist.

✓ *Attach* crystals to red or pink ribbon and hang them in the corners of your home to draw out and fend off negative energies (more about this in the following section).

There really is no right or wrong way to clear your home. The only essential ingredient is the intention to clear your home of any old, outdated, limiting, or negative energies that may be preventing love from finding its way to your door. Once your home is free from unwanted clutter and obstructions, you can employ some basic Feng Shui principles to transform it into a sanctuary of vibrant, attractive, positive energy.

USING FENG SHUI TO MANIFEST YOUR SOULMATE

Feng Shui is the Chinese art of creating harmonious environments. Because it is a four-thousand-year-old tradition that has been handed down through generations, several different adaptations of the art are practiced today, including the Form School, the Compass School, the Black Hat Sect, Intuitive Feng Shui, and many others. However, the essence and underlying intent of all these schools of thought is the same: to create a more positive flow of energy throughout your home. In this section, I will share with you the Feng Shui principles that helped me to attract my soulmate. When taking these steps, I pulled from different sources, including my own intuition. I invite you to experiment with these suggestions, incorporating into your life what you find useful. Ultimately, you must be your own authority and do what feels right to you. In my experience, it's the intention—more than the precise execution—of these principles that draws love into your life.

I first became a believer in Feng Shui more than twenty years ago when I moved into a new home in a new city. I consulted with Feng Shui master Louis Audet and asked his advice on everything from which room to use as my office to where I should place the furniture, mirrors, plants, artwork, bells, chimes, and so forth. Within months of moving into this home and following his recommendations, I watched my career and finances skyrocket.

Later, I met Shawne Mitchell, a leading Feng Shui consultant and author of several books on the subject, who confirmed Louis's recommendations and shared some additional insights about using Feng Shui to attract love. Within two years of applying these principles in my home, I met my soulmate. I don't claim to understand how it works, but the fact remains that it's worked for me (and for most of my friends). As a result, I am a firm believer in utilizing Feng Shui when preparing to manifest a soulmate.

In Feng Shui each section of your home—and each section of every room—is believed to correspond with a specific aspect of your life experience. Each area of your home can be mapped, using a template called the bagua, pictured on page 70. There are eight areas in all, which include *Wisdom and Self-Knowledge*, *Career*, *Helpful People and Travel*, *Children and Creativity*, *Fame and Reputation*, *Wealth and Prosperity*, *Health and Family*, and, of course, the area of *Marriage and Relationships*, which we'll be focusing on in this section.

The first thing you must do is locate the Marriage and Relationships area of your home and the Marriage and Relationships corner of your bedroom. According to the system of Feng Shui that I used, this is how to find these important places in your home:

• • •

Stand at your front door facing into your home, and use the bagua map to locate where the different parts of your room fall within the bagua template. The *far-right corner* is the Marriage and Relationships corner of your entire home.

Next, stand at the doorway of your bedroom facing into that room. The *far-right corner* is the Marriage and Relationships corner of your bedroom.

It's recommended that you concentrate your efforts in both these areas—the Marriage and Relationships corner of your home as well as the Marriage and Relationships corner of your bedroom. Here are some of the best tips I've found for energizing the chi (or energy) in the Marriage and Relationships area of your home or bedroom:

✓ *Decorate* the corner of the room with pink quartz crystals, especially heart-shaped ones. Hang them on pink or red ribbons in the Marriage and Relationships corner of your bedroom or in nearby windows.

✓ *Feature* pictures of animal couples such as swans, cranes (which both mate for life, by the way), dolphins, or doves. Or, if you prefer, a sculpture of a loving couple or family will work well.

✓ *Decorate* this area with abundant red, pink, or peach-colored candles.

✓ *Accessorize* your room with lush green plants—especially those that have heart-shaped leaves.

✓ *Hang* wind chimes in the corner.

✓ *You* may also want to add a work of art on the south wall of your bedroom—something that inspires romance in your heart and provides an uplifting image to focus on. Fresh flowers symbolize growth and expansion and will be a constant reminder to keep your heart open, but avoid keeping dried flowers in your home or bedroom, as they are considered representative of dead energy.

In the process of using Feng Shui to attract your soulmate, one more area of your home deserves mentioning, and that is the Helpful People and Travel section, located in the lower right-hand corner of the bagua, adjacent to the Marriage and Relationships corner of your home. According to Feng Shui principles, by enhancing the flow of chi in this area, you open yourself to receiving help or guidance from unexpected sources. A friend of mine, Gigi, certainly found this to be true.

Feeling a strong desire to meet her soulmate, Gigi did everything in her power to meet him—she said prayers, went to places where singles congregate, and started stopping with friends to have drinks after work—all to no avail. Around this same time, Gigi's friend, Patricia, had been studying Feng Shui and asked if she could practice her newfound skills by doing a consultation on Gigi's house. Gigi was skeptical at first but figured, why not?

As Patricia went through Gigi's home room by room, she discovered many areas that could be enhanced in order to im-

prove her love life. For example, the Marriage and Relationship corner of Gigi's home contained many plants. Patricia
suggested that Gigi put a few of them in red pots (red is an
attractive color and also the color of love), say a prayer three
times as she placed the potted plants back in the room, and
envision what she wanted in the area of her love life. Gigi felt
a little silly but did it anyway, envisioning herself in a wedding
gown, kissing her new groom.

Patricia also noticed that the Helpful People and Travel
section of Gigi's home was barren and poorly lit. Patricia explained that helpful people aren't just those who give you
money, but people who help you in any way—with a word of
wisdom, an introduction to someone special—whatever. Since
so many soulmates find one another thanks to an introduction
by a friend, family member, co-worker, or other such helpful
person, Patricia emphasized the importance of cultivating this
area of Gigi's home and recommended that she place something black in that area and improve the lighting. The next day,
Gigi went out and bought a black halogen torchère, assembled
it that very night, and placed it in the Helpful People and Travel
area. She said a prayer three times and visualized help flowing
to her from all directions.

Mind you, that was on a Friday.

Saturday evening, Gigi's phone rang. It was a co-worker
whom she liked a lot but had never really socialized with beyond walking together at lunchtime or meeting at company

gatherings. The co-worker had called to tell Gigi that her husband's best friend, Rick, had recently gotten divorced and was interested in meeting someone new. Gigi's co-worker explained that she and her husband had been going through their list of available women they knew, when suddenly, like a bolt of halogen lighting, Gigi's name popped into her head. They went out as a foursome the following weekend, and Rick and Gigi have been dating ever since.

In Feng Shui, your bedroom is a place that promotes a harmonious flow of nourishing and sensual energy. Ideally, it should be inviting and soothing, exciting and calming at the same time. Here are a few tips that most experts agree will help you transform your bedroom into a pleasurable and restful place to be:

Transform Your Bedroom

✓ *Bedrooms* should ideally be located in the back of the house in order to provide their inhabitants with a sense of security, privacy, and comfort.

✓ *Avoid* hanging pictures of children or family in a master bedroom, as no one wants to have family members symbolically watching what's going on in the privacy of this space!

✓ *If possible,* don't use your bedroom for an office. Remove all reminders of work, including desks, bookshelves, computers, exercise equipment, and so forth. Remember, your bedroom is a sacred place for sleeping, relaxing, romance, and lovemaking. The fewer distractions, the better.

✓ *It's* not a good idea to keep a television in the bedroom. If you must have a television, put it in a cabinet or cover it with a cloth so you can symbolically make it disappear when it's not in use.

✓ *Choose* the images and artwork you display in your bedroom wisely, and favor images of things you want to experience more of in your life. In other words, unless you enjoy being sad and lonely, do not feature sad and lonely images in your bedroom.

✓ *Avoid* placing mirrors in the bedroom (according to Feng Shui, they are great for the living room but may keep you awake and wired when used in your bedroom).

✓ *Keep* the space under your bed completely free of items. Find alternate storage solutions for winter clothes and extra blankets so you can keep the space around your bed open to receive new vital energy.

✓ *Open* the windows often to keep the air in your bedroom fresh and full of oxygen.

✓ *If* at all possible, make sure your bed is not placed under a window, and ensure that your head is not against a bathroom wall, as those can be inauspicious locations.

Another extremely effective tool for drawing more love into your life is to create what I call a relationship altar. In her book *Creating Home Sanctuaries with Feng Shui*, my friend Shawne Mitchell explains, "Altars have always been used to attract the purest and most revered forces, like a lightning rod." A relationship altar, as I'm defining it here, is simply a collection of images and symbols that conjure feelings of love within you and inspire soulmate success. If you plan to have children, your altar can include photos of happy families or fertility symbols. If travel is important to you, include pictures of exotic locations that you'd like to visit with your beloved. To me, butterflies have always represented creativity—an attribute I wanted to experience with my soulmate—so I built my love altar with photos of butterflies all around. I also included an icon of Krishna and Radha, who represent sacred love, as well as a photo of the Indian saint Amma (who ended up playing a key role in the manifestation of my soulmate).

The purpose of building a relationship altar is twofold: First, it provides a beautiful visual addition to your home or bedroom. Second, and more important, it serves as a focal point to help you clarify and magnetize exactly what you want in a relationship. Of course, you get to decide how simple or elaborate to make your altar and whether to position it in a common area of your home or in the privacy of your bedroom. Use the following suggestions to guide you, but make this process your own by engaging your own creativity:

✓ *Use* the bagua map on page 70 to locate the Marriage and Relationship corner of your home or bedroom, and position your altar in a quiet, out-of-the-way place.

Building a Relationship Altar

✓ *Select* a tabletop that's suitable to the amount of space you have available. A low table covered with a pretty scarf works nicely.

✓ *Decorate* your altar with the photos, symbols, sculptures, or statues that evoke feelings of true love and represent the kind of committed relationship you are seeking. Add pink or red candles and fresh flowers.

✓ *Consider* getting your Treasure Map (described in chapter 1) framed, and hang it directly above your altar—an energetic double whammy!

Remember to have fun with this process and to make it your own by adding colors, textures, images, and items that are close to your heart.

• • •

By following the suggestions in this chapter—removing clutter, purifying the energy of your home, and using centuries-old Feng Shui principles to enliven the flow of vital energy throughout your living space—you are transforming your home into a clear, receptive, and attractive place for love to blossom. Spend some time each day in gratitude and silence, enjoying the space you've created and imagining your heart energetically touching the heart of your soulmate.

Hopefully you are now inspired to transform your home into what I like to call "a soft place to land." This refers to both the physical environment of our homes as well as the emotional places within our hearts. A soft place to land is ultimately what we are looking for in an intimate relationship. And by creating a space in your home right now that you can retreat to, you are in a very tangible sense giving yourself what you are looking for in a relationship. Your soft place to land can be as simple as a comfy oversized chair in the corner of a room or a soft hammock for two under a tree in your backyard. Use this space on a daily basis to focus your attention on your intention to magnetize BIG LOVE, to read your Soulmate List (which you will learn about in chapter 5), or to recite the following prayer, which I used daily and have shared with hundreds of people over the years. When saying this prayer, make sure you are in a quiet, peaceful state where you are simply offering gratitude for what you know is already so. Light a candle, sprawl out on your big beautiful bed, feel your home, your life, and your heart as a soft place for your soulmate to land, and allow each word to ripple through you as you read it aloud:

A DAILY PRAYER FOR MANIFESTING YOUR SOULMATE

God/Goddess and All That Is,
In this moment I am grateful
for the healing of my heart
of everything that would stop me
from attracting my soulmate.
In this moment I remember that my perfect,
right partner is magnetizing to me, and my only
job is to rest in perfect awareness that my soulmate's
heart is already joined with mine as I
"savor the waiting."
And so it is.

CHAPTER FOUR

living as if

...

Do you love me because I am beautiful,
or am I beautiful because you love me?

Cinderella

In the movie *Conversations with God,* the character Neale says to God, "I just want my life back," to which God responds, "You can't *have* anything that you *want*." They then have an entire dialogue where God explains to Neale that by "wanting" something (or someone), all you get is the experience and the feeling of "wanting. "

Now, don't get me wrong, I know you *want* to meet your soulmate—that's a given. In fact, the wanting you feel is a powerful force that sets the process of manifestation into motion. But if what God said to Neale is true—that wanting only produces more wanting—then once we've identified what it is we want, we must learn how to shift our state from wanting it to having it. In the simplest terms, this is the process of living as *if.*

Living as if means stepping outside of your current reality and stepping into the reality you wish to be true. It's when your daily actions reflect and are congruent with your belief that your soulmate exists and is already yours. The best example of this principle I ever heard was told to me by a famous actress (whose identity I unfortunately can't reveal because she swore me to secrecy). Once she became clear that she was ready to share her life with someone, she began living as if that person were already a part of her life. She would play music she imagined he would enjoy; she wore pretty nightgowns to bed instead of her typical T-shirt and sweats. Every morning she would feel that they were waking up and starting their day together, and every night at dinner she would light candles and set a place for him at the table. According to this actress, he eventually arrived. She sent a clear message to the Universe, and the Universe delivered.

Now you may not be willing to set a table for two each night when you have dinner, but start to consider what you could do to generate the feeling that you are already sharing your life with your beloved. For example, buy tickets to a concert or play that is several months away, holding the intention that you will attend it with a hot date. Or the next time you are shopping for greeting cards, pick up a couple that would be fitting to give to your beloved on a birthday or to celebrate your anniversary, knowing that sometime soon that day will be here.

Are there things for your home you are waiting to buy (or are hoping you'll receive as wedding gifts)? Buy them now! If you knew with absolute certainty that your prince or princess would be walking through your front door within a matter of months or weeks, what would you need to do to prepare your home? Would you buy new sheets, towels, or dishes? Clean your bathroom? Plant a garden? You'll know you really, really believe your soulmate is on the way when creating the space for that person in all areas of your life becomes a priority.

I remember when I bought my first condo. I was in my thirties and felt more than a bit conflicted, because I'd always imagined I would be buying my first home with my husband. However, it was the right time financially for me to invest in a home, so I knew I should move forward. Sleeping there alone the first few nights was rough and brought up feelings of longing and sadness. I was definitely in more of a place of *wanting* than a place of *having*. Knowing that this state of being wasn't serving me, I decided to transform my new space into a "love palace" that would evoke feelings of love, warmth, romance, and joyful anticipation of my beloved every time I walked through the door. I had the whole place—including the ceiling—painted a soft pastel pink and furnished it with lush green plants and oversized white furniture you could just sink into. Instead of feeling cold and lonely, my home became a cozy, inviting nest I was proud to wake up to and prouder still to share with someone else.

When you live as if what you want is already your reality, you gain a whole new perspective on your life. Back in the 1970s, when the human-potential movement was just beginning to emerge, research revealed that the human nervous system can't tell the difference between a real event and an imagined

> Love takes off masks that we fear we cannot live without and know we cannot live within.
>
> *James Baldwin*

event. Conjuring the sensations of what it will be like to share your life with another not only changes the way you feel, it can alter your attitude, your posture, and even guide you toward new behaviors. Just for fun, try this experiment: Think of a positive quality you would like to express more of in your life—it might be confidence or patience or sexiness or humor. Now think of someone (it could be someone you know, like a friend or family member, or someone you don't know, like a celebrity) who really embodies that quality. Take a deep breath and imagine physically stepping into this person so you are now looking at the world through that person's eyes. You are seeing the world through the filter of this person's thoughts and beliefs. Does it look any different? Do you feel any different? If you felt this way all the time, would you be inspired to take different actions?

The period of time when you are waiting for your soulmate to make his or her presence known to you gives you an important opportunity for self-reflection. Consider this: if your soulmate had the ability to see your life right now, would you (and your soulmate) be happy with what you're both observing? Begin to live your life today *as if* your soulmate were already here. This is the secret to activating the Law of Attraction! Chances are, if you really knew your soulmate was on his or her way to you, you would hold yourself to a higher standard than you do now—so why wait for that person to arrive to put these things in place? Think not only about what you do on a given day but also the way you represent yourself to others. Now is the time to stop complaining that "all the good ones are taken" and by all means to stop referring to yourself as a "diehard bachelor," a "spinster," or in any similarly derogatory terms. Remember, you will attract someone who energetically matches the degree of esteem you have for yourself. If you are engaging in behaviors you wouldn't want your future lover to see, stop them. This might mean giving up obsessing over your ex-lover or having casual sex with your neighbor.

Six months before I met my soulmate, I met a man I will call Bill. We had this very intense chemistry, but I knew immediately upon meeting him that he was not The One. I had heard plenty about his reputation as a "player," and I knew I didn't want to waste my time and energy on him. But Bill was very charming and cute, and he seemed to always show up whenever I went out with friends. Bill made it very clear he was willing and available to have a fling with me, and he flirted with me like crazy. There were times when I almost said yes . . . but then I realized the Universe was testing me. Saying yes to Bill would have been like saying yes to a hot fudge sundae when I was on a diet. It would have been momentarily pleasurable, but I knew I would regret it immediately afterward. I chose instead to "savor the waiting" and focus on magnetizing my soulmate to me rather than losing sight of my ultimate desire. It wasn't easy, but I was really proud of myself for not giving in to temptation.

I do want to underline something here: the technique of living as if should not be applied like a band-aid to cover over feelings of depression—that will only breed denial. It's important to acknowledge that you will probably go through periods of time when you feel down or even depressed about the fact that you are wanting but not having. I recommend that you surrender to these feelings if and when they arise. Give yourself five minutes to be as depressed as you want to be. Imagine yourself at the bottom of the deepest, darkest, bleakest hole, and write in your journal or even vent out loud about how miserable you are and how empty your life is. Get into it completely. If you want to go for extra credit, do this while looking in the mirror. My prediction is that you will barely be able to stand it for five minutes, and then you'll be ready to move on to a more productive frame of mind. After you've purged your sadness, settle down to an uplifting movie and watch it with the intention of filling yourself up with love, hope, and faith. Some of my favorite love stories of all time include *Pretty Woman*, *Moonstruck*, *Love Actually*, and the classic *Somewhere in Time*.

Remember, the process of attracting your soulmate is magnetism. When you make the choice to live as if your soulmate were already a part of your life, you send out an irresistible signal to the Universe that you are ready *now*. Not a signal that you'll be ready someday—when you work less and your house is clean and you've lost five pounds! Remember the famous line in the 1989 movie *Field of Dreams*, starring Kevin Costner? "If you build it, they will come." Living as if is like flipping on a light switch inside your heart. This is the light your beloved will use to navigate his or her way to your door.

The next feelingization will show you how to turn on your internal heart light so you can send out a clear signal to the Universe that you are ready to receive the love that is already yours.

—Feelingization—
Turning On Your Heart Light

Gently close your eyes and breathe in through your nose and feel yourself letting go of the stresses of your day. As you slowly breathe in and out, allow yourself to settle into your body as the chatter of your mind begins to fade away. Give yourself permission to drop completely into this moment.

As you grow more quiet, more still, and more peaceful, I want you to remember a time when you experienced love or appreciation. This could be something as simple as when you looked into the eyes of a baby, or a pet, or a cherished friend. Allow yourself, in this moment, to re-experience those feelings of love and appreciation . . . and as you do this, place your attention on the area around your heart, and notice that it is beginning to expand. Breathe these feelings of remembered love and appreciation into the area in and around your heart.

Now I want you to imagine that the feelings of love and appreciation you are experiencing are allowing you to locate your own personal heart light. However this appears to you is just perfect. You might see it as a light switch, a torch, a lantern, or even a GPS device. You might just feel it as a sensation of tingling or heat. Whatever works for you, and however you think of it, know that you have an internal heart light. See it now; feel it now . . . and now reach your hand out and switch it to On. Take a breath into your heart as you continue remembering the feelings of love and appreciation, allowing them to grow stronger and stronger.

As you allow yourself to breathe in these feelings, surrender any doubt or thoughts that you are imagining this.

Strongly connected to your internal heart light, imagine now that you can broadcast these feelings of love and appreciation out into the world—out to every other heart in the world—to every man, woman, child, dolphin, bird, every sentient being. Practice broadcasting your purest love to the world, and as you do this, as you are turning your inner heart light to On, know that you are beaming a signal to the heart of your soulmate that you are ready and willing to magnetize him or her into your world.

Continue to see this light emanating from your heart, this light filled with trust and knowingness; see it filling the spaces around your body and beaming out to the world around you. . . . Breathe into this light, into this loving feeling, and continue to send it out to the farthest reaches of the Universe.

Sink into the deep knowingness that your soulmate has been touched, just now, by the energy of your heart. Breathe into the deep knowingness that he or she *is* on the way. Rest assured that every cell of your being now knows that your soulmate is on the way.

You do not need to know the when, the where, or the how of your meeting. . . . Just rest in the *yes* that your soulmate is indeed coming to you. And allow that thought to bring a smile across your lips.

Tell yourself now that it is safe to keep your heart light on. Affirm to yourself that you are loved and protected and ready. Remember that you have much love to give and much love to receive. And know also that as you live as if your soulmate were already with you, you can give your love to everyone you meet. As you do this, your heart light beams stronger and brighter with each loving thought you have.

When you are ready, open your eyes, remembering to keep your heart open as you do.

• • •

To magnetize someone into your life who will love, cherish, and adore you, you first have to become your own biggest fan. This means if you want to attract someone who will romance you, start romancing yourself! If you're looking forward to the day you have that special someone to share joy and adventure with, create some joyful adventures for yourself right now. Before I met Brian, I would sometimes imagine that my soulmate and I would learn to scuba dive together. Eventually, I got tired of waiting and signed up for a scuba-diving course. Once I was certified, I made plans to go on a big diving trip to the Caribbean with a group of women I had met in the course. The moment I set these plans into motion, a man I had been casually seeing for a couple of weeks suddenly became intensely interested in me, moving heaven and earth to go with me on the trip.

Although this man did not turn out to be The One, the way he responded to my decision became an affirmation that I was on the right track. Living as if is a statement to the Universe that you're not willing to postpone your joy to some distant time in the future. The more you live each day as if you were already deeply and passionately in love, the easier it becomes for love to find you.

CHAPTER FIVE

the list

...

*The day will come when, after
harnessing space, the winds, the tides,
and gravitation, we shall
harness for God the energies of love.
And on that day, for the second time
in the history of the world,
we shall have discovered fire.*

Pierre Teilhard de Chardin

When you walk into your favorite coffee hangout, what is the first thing you do? Place your order, of course! You confidently tell the barista, "I will have a tall, half-caff, low-fat mocha latte with a splash of nonsugar vanilla syrup to go." The barista smiles, writes your order on the side of a cup, and takes your money. Within minutes you are walking out the door with the precise, delicious cup of coffee you ordered.

Ordering up a soulmate from the Universe works in a similar way. It's not always as instantaneous, but it can be just as precise. And here is the key to unlocking the full manifestation powers of the Universe: You must *clearly* place your order.

Of course, placing an order for the love of your life demands a bit more thought than ordering up your favorite coffee drink. To do it correctly, you must first search your heart to discover what you really, really desire. I'm sure by now you probably know what you *don't* want in a partner, but attracting your soulmate doesn't work that way. You must ask for what you *do* want.

And the clearer and more specific you are when you ask, the easier it will be for the Universe to answer your call.

Now is the time to deeply and honestly consider your unique goals, desires, tastes, and preferences. As you become clear about what is really important to you in every area of your life, you'll begin to send out a strong and consistent signal that will draw to you a partner who has values and goals that are similar to yours. If, however, you allow yourself to linger too long in ambiguity or get caught in the trap of "keeping all your options open," you may confuse the Cosmic Order Taker as to what it is you really want.

I recently coached a forty-five-year-old woman named Colleen who had been looking to meet her soulmate for most of her adult life. I began by trying to elicit from her exactly what she was looking for in a man and what kind of lifestyle she envisioned creating with him. I asked her what I considered to be a pretty straightforward question—do you want kids?—and was surprised when she couldn't give me a clear answer. After some probing, I discovered that she really didn't relish the idea of raising someone else's young children but felt that if she wasn't willing to compromise, she would further reduce her odds of meeting someone of similar age and interests. One part of her knew that the lifestyle she longed for did not include children, yet another part of her was afraid to admit it. How clear a signal do you think she was sending out to the Universe? By hedging her bets, Colleen was not only compromising her wishes but was also making it extremely difficult for the Universe to bring her an exact match.

COMPROMISES AND DEAL BREAKERS

As my husband, Brian, and I were having dinner the other night, I began telling him about a blind date our friend Roberta had recently been on. Apparently her date had a most unpleasant habit, of which he seemed to be completely unaware. According to Roberta, he was constantly making strange sucking sounds with his mouth, even when he wasn't eating. When I relayed this story to Brian, he looked up from his meal, set his fork down, and stared me directly in the eyes. "Well," he said, matter-of-factly. "*That's* a deal breaker."

Each of us has a unique set of preferences and standards, and what is completely acceptable to one person could be a deal breaker for another. A certain degree of compromise is to be expected in every relationship, and I'm certainly not suggesting that you and your soulmate will live happily ever after without having to make a single adjustment. Compromising and accommodating to another person's needs are a part of growth, both as a couple and as individuals. However, if you find that being with a particular person means having to compromise one or more of your core values, I would suggest that he or she is probably not the person for you. If you know you absolutely want children and you meet someone who absolutely does not, that's a deal breaker. Making your Soulmate List is a great way to clarify your important values, and the clearer you are before you meet your soulmate, the easier it will be to recognize The One.

GOD IS IN THE DETAILS

Once you're clear about which characteristics you're willing to compromise on and which you are not, you are ready to create your list. Begin by thinking about the aspects of your life that you look forward to sharing with a partner, the things you look forward to doing together, and the way you would like to feel in his or her presence. Here are some specific questions, the answers to which will provide essential information that will help you create and refine your list:

1 How would I like to feel when I wake up in the morning next to my soulmate?_____

_____

_____

2 What kind of lifestyle will we lead? Are we both worka-holics or couch potatoes or a combination of the two?

_____

_____

3 How will we spend our weekends? Hiking local trails, taking in movies or cultural events, or hanging out around the house?_____

_____

_____

4 Do we have or want children, and am I willing to accept someone else's children into my life?_____

_____

_____

Telling the Universe the characteristics you are looking for in a soulmate is similar to typing a keyword into an Internet search engine. The more specific you are, the greater the chances your search will yield exactly what you're looking for. You are placing a very specific order with the Universe, so as you're writing your list, make sure it includes two important criteria:

1 My soulmate is single, straight/gay (yes, you must be that specific), and available for a healthy, loving, committed, long-term relationship (or marriage if that is what you want).

2 My soulmate is someone who lives within __ miles of me or is willing to move here.

> Love is the triumph
>
> of imagination over
>
> intelligence.
>
> *H. L. Mencken*

If you are willing to move to be near your soulmate but want to live in a certain state or country, specify that as well.

I know people who have made Soulmate Lists and then met the person of their dreams—only to discover the person they manifested has a different sexual orientation and/or lives on the other side of the planet. I had one friend—let's call her Lori—who was certain she had met the love of her life. He met the criteria on her list in every way—except he was gay. She was so in love with him that she was convinced she could change him. Of course, she couldn't and didn't, and it took her a long time to finally let go. I also met a woman who manifested her perfect soulmate except that she was happily settled in Dayton, Ohio, and he lived in Sydney, Australia. The point here is that you need to be clear and very specific when placing your order with the Universe to deliver your soulmate.

Of course, there is a point at which we can take specificity a bit too far. I met a woman once who had such specific ideas about the type of man she wanted to marry that she literally refused to date anyone with anything above a thirty-two-inch waist! She became obsessed with this one specific detail and blocked out anything and anyone who didn't match it. This woman did, by the way, end up with a man who met her very specific criteria. He was a nail-biting cheapskate, but he did have a thirty-two-inch waist. It's far more important that you clarify the inner characteristics you want in a partner than hold out for someone who has a specific physical characteristic. There are exceptions to this, of course, and sometimes it happens that a particular physical characteristic actually helps you to recognize your soulmate when you meet him or her.

When I first created my soulmate list, it was really long and specified something like forty-eight items. One of the things that spontaneously came forth when I put my pen to the page was that my soulmate would have grey hair. I never really understood why—and grey hair had not been important to me up until that point—but I just had this idea he should have grey hair. Sure enough, when I met Brian, he not only had grey hair (his hair turned grey while he was in his early thirties), he also had every quality on my list except two: he wasn't Jewish and he doesn't cook. These two items turned out not to be deal breakers after all, since I am not a practicing Jew, and suffice it to say we have never missed a meal.

RELEASE YOUR EXPECTATIONS

The Rolling Stones had it figured out decades ago when they told us, "You can't always get what you want." Sometimes we have to let go of what we think we want in order to make space for the Universe to deliver what we need. There is a fine line between clarifying what we want (love, happiness, fulfillment) and becoming rigidly attached to our wishes (I need to meet him before Valentine's Day, and he must be at least six feet tall and have brown eyes). The following story is a beautiful testament of what can happen when we release our expectations and let go of our need to be the general manager of the Universe.

Kathi's Story
The Black Hole of My Expectations

Three years after my first marriage ended, I was still alone and had not found my perfect mate. I was dating, going out to nice lunches and lovely dinners, but none of the men met my expectations. I was filled with a longing that left me feeling hollow and unconnected. I was in my midthirties, and time was running out. I wanted children.

I tried lots of things to speed the process. A psychic told me that my future partner's name begins with the initial "B." For several years, I peered hopefully at various Bills and Bobs, but none of them was my soulmate. I made a list of the top ten characteristics of my ideal partner—I remember "playmate" was at the top of the list—and posted it on my refrigerator, where it grew yellow and torn until it fell off and was lost. I practiced celibacy for a while and yoga and took spiritual retreats.

And then two things happened. I got used to spending time by myself and began to enjoy it more. And I went to a wedding.

At the reception, the bride, a young female intern at the TV station where I worked, spontaneously invited me to join her wedding party for a group honeymoon in Mexico. They had chartered a plane, and a single seat had opened up—I could join their party at a fraction of the usual cost and have a lovely getaway in Puerto Vallarta, the gorgeous seaside resort where Elizabeth Taylor and Richard Burton had romanced each other during the filming of *The Night of the Iguana*. On impulse, I decided to go.

It was a disaster. I couldn't keep up with the fun-loving twenty-somethings, who seemed hellbent on personal destruction—never sleeping, smoking cigarettes, and drinking much more than I could. They danced long into the night and laughed at inside jokes I didn't get. I wound up retiring early, spending the following days and evenings on my own, feeling old and very sorry for myself.

My sense of isolation culminated on the last evening, when I walked along the beach at sunset and ended up sitting on a stone wall, taking in the overwhelming beauty of it all. Surrounded by couples and honeymooning lovers, I was miserable, feeling lonely and forsaken. Sitting there, I once again imagined my mysterious Mr. B, drew his outline in my imagination beside me on the wall, and took comfort in that fantasy for a few moments. I thought, *If only he were here beside me, then I would be complete. I would be happy.*

Suddenly, as I turned to look at my imaginary partner, my sense of comfort vanished. The shape of a man I imagined outlined in white beside me turned into a black hole. In that moment, I realized no one could ever fill the ideal outline I had constructed.

Outside the black hole, the colors of the sunset surrounded me. I realized if I couldn't sit there amid that extraordinary beauty and peace and be happy all by myself in the experience, no one was going to be able to do that for me. And if "B" couldn't make me happy, I would blame him for his shortcomings and fall out of love, as I had before.

My sunset epiphany changed my life in that it changed my expectations. I gave them up. I returned home and soon after was cast in a play opposite a man named Byron. We had met in 1985, the year my husband and I separated. He liked me then and even wrote to me to ask me out, but I ignored the letter. I hadn't really noticed him because he didn't fit my imaginary outline of my ideal man.

Without the expectations of who my perfect partner should be and what he would look like, I was able to appreciate the treasure that Byron is. After eight years of getting to know each other, my dear, sweet Mr. B and I were married in 1996. This marriage battlefield has been one of great victories and surrenders for both of us. I recently found the yellowed paper I thought I'd thrown away years ago: my top ten list for my ideal mate. I was amazed how well it described Byron. Not only did I meet him in a play, but he continues to be my best playmate in life.

CREATING YOUR SOULMATE LIST

To get you started, below are a handful of qualities and traits to consider when creating your Soulmate List. Read these for ideas, but write down only the qualities and traits that are really important to you. If you have past lovers with whom you had happy memories (or perhaps you are still friends), think about the qualities you most cherished in them, as it might provide a clue as to the type of person you are ready to manifest now. Take as much time as you need to create your list, and make it as short or long as you like.

Abundant

Adorable

Affectionate

Ambitious

Articulate

Beautiful

Bubbly

Caring

Charismatic

Creative

Considerate

Emotionally available

Endearing

Enjoys _____ (add your choice of words—dogs, cats, travel, chanting, etc)

Family oriented

Flexible

Fun, funny

Generous (you can add:
with money, time, affec-
tion, etc.)

Great relationships
(with family, children,
ex-spouses, etc.)

Happy

Healthy

Independent

Loves to _____(cook,
play golf, bungee jump, or
whatever turns you on)

Loving

Nuturing

Playful

Sexy

Sensuous

Smart

Spiritually open (or attends
church, temple, mosque,
etc.)

Successful

Supportive (of your career,
dreams, triathlon training,
etc.)

Talented

Here is a list one of my friends recently made:

The twenty qualities I would like in my soulmate (in no particular order):

Intelligent

Honest

Loving

Emotionally healthy

Physically healthy

Extremely kind

Abundant

FUN

Self-secure   Giving

Attractive   Compatible

Sweet   Easygoing

Physical/sexual chemistry   Successful

Sense of humor   Grateful

Great communicator

We then rewrote her final list so it read like an affirmation she could repeat to herself each day:

I, Leslie Ann Leeds,* give thanks to God, Goddess, and All That Is for my beloved soulmate. I am grateful he is single, straight, and available for a healthy, loving, committed, lifelong relationship. He lives within fifty miles of San Diego, California, or is very willing to move here. He is an intelligent, honest, loving man who is emotionally and physically healthy. He is an extremely kind, sweet, fun, secure, attractive man with whom I have great sexual chemistry. He is successful, abundant, giving, and easygoing and practices gratitude on a daily basis. He is a great communicator, and we have a happy and comfortable life together. As I savor the waiting for his impending arrival, I relax in the peace and comfort that we will soon be together. And so it is.

*not her real name

Now, if you were the Universe, how could you resist fulfilling such a beautiful order? Once you have your list, you should then have a trusted friend review it with you to make sure you haven't forgotten anything critical. In Leslie's case she is not looking for marriage or children, so that has been left out. If you desire marriage and/or children, remember to specifically ask for that. You may think you already know what you want, but the moment you articulate your desires with clarity, specificity, and feeling, you increase the magnetic pull between you and your beloved by at least a hundredfold. In fact, the act of writing down the qualities you most desire in a soulmate may lead you to the realization that this person is closer than you think. Such was the case for entrepreneur and bestselling author John Assaraf.

John's Story
The Third Time's a Charm

Ever since I can remember, I have wanted to be in a loving, caring, honest, and fulfilling relationship. Throughout my teens and early twenties, I had heard the term "soulmates," but I certainly didn't have any role models who embodied that kind of love. None of my friends' parents seemed to be really connected, and my own parents were more like housemates than soulmates. Like many people of that era, they got married at a very young age because when you dated and were intimate with someone, marriage was a foregone conclusion. Although

I received a lot of love as a child, what I learned about intimate relationships from my parents would end up costing me a lot—emotionally as well as financially.

My first marriage was to a really wonderful gal. We had a lot of fun together, but like my parents, we got married for all the wrong reasons. A year after we began dating, I moved away from Toronto, where we had met, to build my first company. For two years she flew back and forth between Indiana and Toronto so we could continue our relationship. One weekend she gave me an ultimatum: If we didn't get married, the relationship would be over. Based on that and my belief that it was the right thing to do, I agreed and we got married. Then everything changed. Our relationship up to that point had been pretty superficial, and we had never gotten into all the very important discussions about life, purpose, ambitions, and our individual goals and dreams. Still, we dove into the marriage as if we were playing roles in a movie. While I was building my company, working eighty hours a week, she was bored silly. In addition, because she was a Canadian citizen, she could not work in the States. After two years of desperately trying and pretending to make it work, I decided it was best if we parted ways. In retrospect, we were young and probably more in lust than deeply in love. The idea of marriage was compelling for both of us, and I think we fell in love with the idea of being in love.

Within very short order after our divorce, I met a spunky twenty-two-year-old (I was thirty at the time) with whom I had a lot of fun. I had no intention of getting married again—that is until she got pregnant and neither of us wanted to have a child out of wedlock. Somehow, I rationalized that because we were having fun, we would also be able to raise a child and make our relationship work. We couldn't. Almost immediately after we got married and our first child was born, we discovered how very different we were. Fortunately for me, we brought another wonderful child into the world before we mutually decided that while we cared for each other and wanted to lovingly coparent our children, we should not be married. For a second time I found myself divorced and feeling like a total failure in relationships.

Here I was, fairly successful in most areas of my life, making what I believed to be all the right decisions, but finding my soulmate was proving to be as elusive as finding the Holy Grail. What I didn't realize at the time was that both my strategy for attracting love and my decision-making process were flawed. In business and in other areas of my life, I would set very specific, clear goals with as much detail as possible, yet in the area of relationships I was settling for what circumstances provided me.

I decided to be single for as long as it took to heal from the pain of two divorces as well as to understand my part in the breakdown of both my marriages. After a lot of reflection, I saw that when it came to love, I was very immature, hardheaded, and thought I knew it all. The truth is, I knew nothing about what it took to be a great partner, and I had no idea what I really wanted in a soulmate. For the first time, I realized what a limited and shallow understanding I had of love and relationships. I also realized I was emulating my father.

This new awareness led me to two important decisions. First, I was going to invest as much effort in learning how to be a great partner as I had invested in building my companies; and second, I was going to apply the Law of Attraction to find my perfect partner.

One day as I was revisiting my life's goals, I wrote a very detailed description of what I wanted my soulmate to be like. As I wrote, I described every detail: her personality, smile, demeanor, likes, dislikes, passions, sexuality, family, religious views, travel desires, and everything else I could think of that represented my ideal partner and soulmate. After writing my list and tweaking it to perfection, I filed it away in my goal-setting manual and left it alone. I had trusted the Universe to fufill my desires in other areas of my life and saw no reason to doubt that it would work in love. In other words, I had total faith in the power that gives us life finding my soulmate without imposing effort or timelines.

Early one Saturday morning I was riding a stationary bike at the gym and talking to a dear friend, when two stunning women walked into the gym. I quickly pointed them out to my friend, and we chuckled at the fact that he and I were never single at the same time. Leaving my friend to finish his workout without me, I walked downstairs and casually introduced myself to this lovely woman whom I found irresistibly beautiful. We chatted briefly, and I asked her about where to eat and what to do in San Diego, as I had just moved there from Los Angeles. She told me she and a bunch of people got together most weekends at a certain location at the beach. The following weekend I took my two boys to the exact location she described, and wouldn't you know it . . . she showed up an hour after we got there. That was the beginning of a wonderful on-again, off-again relationship that lasted six years. I wasn't ready to make a matrimonial commitment, and I was very clear with her about that from the beginning.

One day while I was going through my goal-setting folder, I found the list I had written years earlier detailing the perfect soulmate for me. When I read it, it became very clear to me that I had already met my soulmate and didn't even realize it. A hundred percent of what I wrote precisely described the woman I was currently dating. Needless to say, I asked her to marry me, and fortunately she said yes. After we were married, I showed Maria the list I had written years before, and she could hardly believe it. We were both shocked at the details and the accuracy of the description. Our relationship has continued to flourish over the years, and we are both firm believers in the Law of Attraction.

• • •

After you've contemplated the specific qualities that are important to you in a partner, write your list out in ink on a beautiful sheet of stationery. As you write each word, imagine you are living with your soulmate right now, giving thanks for his or her presence in your life. Enjoy the feelings of joy, happiness, passion, and peace that come with knowing you and your soulmate have found each other at last.

Now that you've created your list, it's important to release it with a sacred ceremony. By symbolically releasing it, you are surrendering your attachment to how, where, and when your soulmate will arrive, and you're allowing the Universe to handle the details. As Deepak Chopra writes in *The Seven Spiritual Laws of Success*, "In order to acquire anything in the physical universe, you have to relinquish your attachment to it. This doesn't mean you give up the intention to create your desire. . . you give up your attachment to the result."

Pick a special day to perform this ritual, perhaps during a full moon or new moon, on a Friday (the day of Venus, goddess of love) or any other day you deem special. Select a time of day that feels right for you (I released my list at noon on a Friday). Then select a location—perhaps in your newly Feng Shui'd bedroom, in front of your relationship altar, or in a serene spot in nature or in your backyard.

Start by reading your Soulmate List out loud, allowing the feeling of every word, trait, quality, and desire to ripple through you. Then, in an act of faith that your wishes have been heard and granted, put your list into a firesafe container and burn it. As your list is turning to ash, know that your deepest intentions are being handed over to unseen forces that will orchestrate the time and place when you will one day meet your soulmate. Take the ashes and release them into a body of water (the ocean, a river, a lake, etc.), or if that isn't possible or practical, plant them in a garden. Even if you prefer to keep your list for future reference, you can still symbolically release it by storing it away somewhere special.

Take a few minutes to sit quietly with your eyes closed, feeling your heart opening and expanding and knowing that your prayers have been released to the powers of the Universe. In the quiet of your heart, send a message to your beloved that you are looking forward to seeing him or her soon.

If burning your list doesn't appeal to you, you can read it out loud and then fold it into a small bundle and tie it to a red or pink helium balloon. Take the balloon to a beautiful open space and set it free. As the balloon soars high into the sky, know that your prayers are on their way to being answered. Or you can do what my friend Danielle did and place your list in a sealed envelope under your mattress, mischievously anticipating the day she would share it with her beloved.

You can also rewrite your list as an affirmation (like Leslie did on page 107) and place it on your relationship altar.

The last phase of your Soulmate List ritual is to create a private celebration. It can be as simple as enjoying a glass of champagne at an elegant location while you practice beaming love to everyone you see, or you may want to cook a delicious meal, set the table for two, light candles, play romantic music, and bask in the knowingness that the wheels of destiny have been set into motion for you and your beloved. Whatever kind of celebration feels right to you will be perfect.

MAKE THIS PROCESS YOUR OWN

Some people find the act of writing a list of their soulmate's characteristics a bit too formal or left-brained. If you are more the creative type who thinks in a nonlinear way, you may find coloring, drawing, or doodling your soulmate's attributes an easier way to tap into your heart's desires. The following story is a beautiful example of allowing your creativity to fill in the blanks.

Gayle's Story
Coloring the Love Mandala

December of 1984. I was twenty-seven and had a creative and stimulating job, working with film and video editors and computer animators. I had a great duplex apartment with a spiral staircase and exposed brick walls in a fun area of Chicago near Lake Michigan. In my spare time I was part of an improvisational comedy troupe and had a group of fun-loving friends. All in all, a great life. But I was so lonely. I longed for a partner, a man who could share my life with me. It seemed like I had exhausted every last option. I had gone out on a blind date with my friend's older brother, a blind date through a business associate, and even a date with a neighbor from another building, but alas, no love connection. I resigned myself to a single life: I would be grateful for all life's gifts and count my blessings even if they didn't include the man of my dreams.

As Christmas and New Year's loomed ahead, I was dateless but not friendless. I occupied my time having dinner with my improv and work pals and spent quiet evenings reading spiritual books and practicing yoga. Late one evening, as I sifted through my astrological reading, I remembered something my astrologer had said to me regarding finding my life partner. She advised me to take a mandala (an intricate design of shapes, usually in a circular pattern) and color each tiny area with colored pencils or markers, vocalizing and meditating about what qualities I would like my future husband to possess.

Lying on my bedroom floor with the mandala in front of me, a rainbow of multicolored pencils fanned around me and the scent of incense from a burning stick of sandalwood wafting in the air, I declared my intention: to find the perfect spiritual friend and lover to go through life with. I selected a beautifully colored pencil and began coloring a tiny section while thinking intently about each individual quality I desired in my future mate. *I would like a man who is kind to animals*, I thought, while coloring a space with violet; *I would like a man who appre-*

ciates my sense of humor, while coloring with periwinkle blue. I thought of each intention and filled the space with a splash of color. A brilliant hue of green for *I want a man who is nice to the waitress or restaurant server*. I chose ruby red for *a man who is accepting and open to my spiritual quest*. On and on, for each new intention a new color. *A man who likes things I like about myself that other people think are weird*. (No, I'm not sharing those qualities with you.) And finally, *A man I can share my dreams with*.

My astrologer said to be very specific. The mandala was becoming a multihued testimony to the qualities I desired in my future partner. I was a little sheepish when I thought, *"I would like a man who has a cute butt*. I didn't feel very spiritual as I colored that section while focusing on that particular intention. (Hey, I was only twenty-seven and still a little shallow.) My finished mandala looked like I was peering through a kaleidoscope: brilliant swirling colors forming a multifaceted gemlike pattern. I had put my request out to the Universe, and it was no longer in my hands.

Christmas passed, and I was faced with New Year's Eve. I had an offer to go out with a perfectly delightful man who wanted to be more than just friends, and I was offered an invitation from a man who only wanted to be friends with me. Neither offer was the ideal scenario. So I just decided to ring in the New Year with good friends. My improv pals were meeting at a local nightclub at 11:00 p.m., and I was grateful to be meeting them rather than coupling up with someone just because it was New Year's Eve.

December 31, 1984, was a very snowy night. I was filled to the brim with healthy New Year's resolutions and decided to go to my health club for a quick workout. I had made peace with my life: I was single, I had great friends, a great life, and a job where I made plenty of money. It didn't matter if I *never* met the man of my dreams. I was satisfied with the life I had created.

I drove my little Nissan Sentra to Chicago's East Bank Club, feeling like a metal ball in a pinball machine, sliding about the street and thankful not to be slamming into the parked cars dusted with snow. Not surprisingly, there were plenty of parking spots near the normally bustling club. Even the woman at the front desk seemed surprised to see a club member working out on such a snowy, wintery New Year's Eve.

Once inside the club, I made a beeline for the stationary bicycles to warm up. I pedaled away, staring blankly ahead and going nowhere fast. The usually busy club was a ghost town. That suited me; I had no makeup on, and my normally perky bob looked like a nest. Suddenly, out of nowhere, an attractive, dark-haired man sat on the Schwinn Aerodyne next to me and began pedaling away. "How long are you riding for?" he asked. I was not in the mood to talk since I was *happy* with my life. "Thirty minutes," I replied. I was truly not interested in talking and seriously hoped he would leave me and my nest-like hairdo alone.

"Great," he said. "I'm riding forty-five." His big brown eyes smiled at me.

As I huffed and puffed, we discussed our New Year's Eve plans. He was going to a party with a friend, and I told him about my rendezvous with pals at eleven. We exchanged names and continued making small talk to the whir of the bicycles. "Well, I'm going to do some stretches. Nice chatting with you," I said, slinking away to a large mirrored studio. I pulled a mat off the stack and started doing a series of yoga stretches, relieved to be alone. *Yikes, this is the last time I ever do a clay mask before I go to the health club,* I thought, gazing at my red face in the mirrors. Shoulder stand, plow, fish pose. A head pokes in through the open wooden doors. "Hey," says big brown eyes, "do you want to get an orange juice after you're done with your workout?" We agreed to meet, after we both showered, in the bar area near the grill.

It's amazing what a great spin a shower and a good blow-dry can put on your attitude. I looked like myself again. I met big-brown-eyes Howard in the grill. We ordered orange juice on the rocks and chatted. He was sweet, sensitive, funny, and very cute. We barely had time to finish our orange juice when they began to close the club for the evening. After exchanging business cards, we agreed to a dinner date on Wednesday.

I drove home in one of the worst snow storms in the history of New Year's Eve in Chicago. The snow was coming down fast and thick, covering my windshield like a blanket. I arrived home and quickly put on my holiday attire for the evening. Taking a taxi seemed safer than maneuvering through the streets in my tiny foreign import. The weather was impossible, the snow was blinding, and there wasn't a taxi or car in sight. I trudged through the snow back to my apartment. The wind howled, and ice crystals pelted the windowpane as I settled in for a steaming cup of herbal tea and an evening of Marx Brothers films.

On Wednesday night, Howard picked me up for our date. He was handsome, laughed at my jokes, and didn't flinch when I talked about meditation. We went to a very hip Tex-Mex place and sat near a kiva fireplace. We talked and talked and talked. We shared a delicious meal and laughed about the paralyzing snow storm of New Year's Eve. He was really sweet and genuinely nice to the server. He loved animals, was passionate about martial arts, had a cat named Wolf, and as a drummer, he was into all types of music. It was a spectacular evening.

We could have talked all night. We were kindred spirits. We both had to work the next day, so we called it a night at 11:30. Howard walked me to my doorway and kissed me goodnight. It was a Great Kiss. I watched him as he walked down the hallway of my apartment building, and you know, of course, he had a great butt. We have been together ever since. He is the man of my dreams. And we are truly soulmates. (You can color your own Mandala; it's on page 209.)

• • •

I love this story because it encapsulates some of the key principles that govern the Law of Attraction: in the process of manifesting her soulmate, Gayle was relaxed, lighthearted, content in her own life, and approaching her soulmate search with a spirit of joyful anticipation rather than of need. This is an important point, because it is not your soulmate's job to save your life, bail you out of debt, or rescue you from your inner demons. Your soulmate is a friend and partner with whom you will share the most intimate aspects of your life, someone who understands the power and beauty of a true soulmate union and will hold the space for love even when you can't. When my friend Maxine was focusing on manifesting her soulmate, her prayer was to "to make someone as happy as I would like to be." Within two hours of saying this prayer, she met the man who became her husband six months later. Today, twelve years later, they are still blissfully in love.

To the best of your ability, be relaxed and lighthearted about your soulmate search. You never doubt that the barista with whom you've placed your latte order will come through for you, and neither should you doubt the Universe's ability to deliver your true love.

CHAPTER SIX

unhooking
the past

...

*Love is that condition in which
the happiness of another person
is essential to your own.*

Robert Heinlein

Remember the old definition of insanity? Albert Einstein described it as doing the same thing over and over again and expecting different results. In trying to manifest your soulmate without first clearing out the emotional and psychic clutter of your past, you run the risk of attracting the same type of person you have failed with in the past. If you are still carrying around any emotional baggage from past relationships (and I'm going to suggest that most of us are), commit right now to working through it. When you have unhooked yourself from the heartaches, resentments, and disappointments of your past, you lay the foundation for a healthy, happy, and fulfilling life with your soulmate.

Let's get clear about one thing right up front: to be human is to be wounded. None of us can escape this simple fact. Whether we endured a difficult childhood, experienced rejection from a hurtful lover, or felt the disappointment of a failed relationship, we all have emotional wounds that are in need of healing.

As you prepare yourself to magnetize your soulmate, you must decide now to actively begin healing the deepest wounds of your heart. Please note that I said *begin* the healing process. For many of us, this may be a lifelong journey, and you don't have to be free of every bit of emotional baggage in order to manifest your soulmate. In fact, one of the things a soulmate does is help you to heal your deepest wounds. Nonetheless, if you are really committed to sending out a clear and pure signal of your readiness to attract a healthy, committed partner, you really do need to clear out the emotional blocks that keep you anchored to the past in a negative way.

Reflect for a moment on the list of qualities and attributes that you are looking for in a lover, then ask yourself if who you are on an emotional level is a good match for the person you described. If the walls around your heart are ten feet thick, you may be unconsciously keeping love at arm's length. A heart that is burdened with old hurts, disappointments, and resentments is simply not open enough to allow love to enter. In fact, your unprocessed or unhealed emotional wounds may be sending the Universe a mixed message. One part of you is a giant *yes* to being in an intimate relationship, while your wounded heart is unconsciously saying, *No, I am afraid of being hurt again*. Your job now is to uncover the wounds and begin the healing process so that you can send a clear signal that you are ready for love. At the heart of this process is forgiveness.

THE POWER OF FORGIVENESS

The other morning I was watching the news on TV and happened to see a segment about a mother whose daughter had been murdered a decade earlier. This woman explained how she had been carrying a huge amount of rage, bitterness, and hatred toward the man who had murdered her daughter (who was then serving a life sentence in a high-security prison). Finally, she decided she could no longer bear living with that much anger, so she wrote the man a letter. In her letter she told him she had finally decided to forgive him. She told the news anchor that the moment the letter went into the mailbox, all her anger and rage evaporated, and she felt the full release of the forgiveness she had just bestowed on this man. She said if she had only known the power of forgiveness, she would have forgiven him years earlier.

Similarly, to release the emotional blocks that keep us from allowing love in, we must call upon the power of forgiveness. In her award-winning book, *Spiritual Divorce*, Debbie Ford, my sister and a bestselling author, explains that "forgiveness is the hallway between the past and the future." Put simply, when we have healed the scars of our pasts, we open the door to a more fulfilling future.

Colette's Story
Healing the Past

My experience with men was abrupt and loveless from the beginning. I lost my virginity in a drunken excursion with a relative stranger on my eighteenth birthday. A year later I found myself at a bar, drunk again, this time accepting a ride home from a group of men I only vaguely knew. What later ensued would color my choices for years, as I experienced the degradation and demoralization of gang rape. The aftermath was devastating, and the men I attracted from that point forward were perfect mirrors of my rage against men and my self-hatred. I found myself in relationship after relationship with angry, rageful, misogynistic men with some combination of sex addiction, drug addiction, alcoholism, and issues with gambling. None of these men treated me with respect because I didn't respect myself. None of them were available to me emotionally because I was unavailable to myself. None of them were faithful because I was always betraying myself. All of them were caught in the same trap of dishonesty and denial as I was.

At twenty-seven, I went into recovery for my addiction to alcohol. I came to believe in a Higher Power. I began to study metaphysics and read book after book about what is now understood as the Law of Attraction. Wallace Wattles, Catherine Ponder, Ernest Holmes, Alice Bailey, Norman Vincent Peale, James Allen, and Shakti Gawain became my bedside-table best friends. I began to use creative visualization, affirmations, and vision boards with artistic collages to help me envision and manifest a loving partner. I created a dream board, cutting out photographs and images from magazines depicting a dark-haired, handsome man. I even went as far as cutting out a picture of a wedding dress. I meditated every day on the physical aspect of this man and the wedding dress and the act of getting married. And yet deep inside I still hadn't forgiven myself or the men who raped me, so it really came as no surprise that the partner I attracted mirrored the lack of love and self-regard I felt toward myself.

I met my first husband on a blind date. He was the spitting image of the handsome man with dark hair on my vision board. He asked me to marry him a short while later. It was a perfect relationship for the space I was in at the time, both energetically and emotionally. We were mutually disrespectful in our language and unavailable to each other, and when all was said and done, both of us were disappointed and disillusioned. As it turned out, this was the best thing that could have happened to me. The light finally went on.

I hit bottom emotionally and finally had to surrender to the fact that I was still full of repressed rage about the rape, that I still considered myself a victim, that I was retaliatory, distrustful, and emotionally unavailable—not only to men but also to myself. That was the beginning of my true healing. I committed to a year of celibacy and introspection in order to unhook myself from the pain of my past, which kept playing out in my present. I learned to forgive, to release my resentments, and to see my role in my life's dramas. Eventually I recovered a sense of hope. Humility quietly took the place of the anger and fear I had harbored for so long. I became the love I had been looking for. I finally forgave myself. At the young age of forty-four I was ready to allow God's will to guide my intimate relationships. I prayed daily for God to decide who my life partner should be, if I was to have one at all. I woke up one morning feeling hopeful again.

Throughout this time, I had been coaching a number of my clients on how to manifest their life partners using the Internet as a meditation tool. I guess it's true that you teach what you most need to learn. My clients were achieving wonderful results, and I thought I should try it myself. I went online the next day to a dating site, and lo and behold an ad popped up of the most beautiful-looking man. I didn't even read his ad. All I had to do was look in his eyes and my intuitive radar went *ping!* I contacted him, he called me back, and the minute I heard his voice I knew he was The One. There was no anxiety, just a calm, welcoming, friendly feeling that was nothing like the romantic yearning I had felt in every other relationship I'd had. We both figured out fairly quickly that we were meant to be together. Since the day we met, we've not been apart.

Because I was emotionally healed and whole, my relationship with my soulmate was built on a sturdy foundation. I made an important commitment right from the start that I would never use a disrespectful word or act in a disrespectful manner toward him. We had both had our share of difficult relationships in the past and knew what we didn't want to repeat. Experience told us both, "If you do what you always did, you're gonna get what you always got!"

Of course, we decided to honor our commitment with vows of the spirit and a legal marriage. When we married, we agreed divorce would never be an option. We always resolve our differences before bed, put each other first, and fully support the other's spiritual and personal growth. There's no manipulation, no struggle for power, and we always stand close together but not so close as to cast a shadow over the other. We're a team. We're best friends. We call each other on our stuff out of love for each other. We laugh together about goofy things. We know we aren't perfect, but we're perfect for each other. I never would have been able to attract such a healthy relationship if I hadn't found forgiveness for myself and for all those I felt had betrayed me.

● ● ●

As Colette Baron-Reid's story powerfully illustrates, forgiveness is a two-part process: first, we must forgive those who have hurt us, and second, we must forgive ourselves for all the times we didn't listen to our intuition or made choices out of desperation, or for any of the hundreds of other things for which we blame ourselves.

FORGIVING YOURSELF

In chapter 2, I encouraged you to write a letter to any past lovers with whom you felt incomplete and to then write a letter to yourself from their perspectives. I hope you did that exercise, because it was the primer for this next one. To take the process of unhooking yourself from the past a step deeper, I invite you to now write a letter of forgiveness to yourself. It's important that you forgive yourself for all the times you allowed yourself to remain in relationships that didn't serve your highest and best good—and it's equally important to put it in writing. Be specific and write out the names of all the people and the specific incidents that have caused your heart to shut down. At the end of each paragraph please add this sentence: *I completely and totally forgive myself for these actions, and I completely and totally forgive* _____*(add names) for their actions. I now bless myself and* ____ *(add names) and gratefully accept this healing of my heart. And so it is.*

When you have finished writing this letter, read it out loud to yourself, allowing yourself to feel the release that forgiveness brings. You may feel a huge opening in your heart, or you may notice just a subtle movement in the direction of forgiveness. Consider reading your forgiveness letter out loud, to yourself, daily for the next ten days. If you feel no movement at all after doing this, you may want to consider getting extra help from a counselor, coach, or therapist. And by the way, if you find that you are resisting doing this exercise, allow yourself to be resistant for a few minutes, and then sit down and do it anyway.

• • •

Here's what you will need to complete the exercise:

A
Forgiveness
Excercise

☐ ten to thirty minutes

☐ stationery and a good working pen

☐ a candle and some soothing music (I prefer Gregorian chants)

☐ willingness to complete the task

☐ willingness to cut the cord and forgive

Once you have forgiven yourself and your past lovers, it is time to gently and lovingly disconnect from them energetically. Many energy workers believe we leave energetic hooks in people with whom we've been intimate. These can be positive hooks—such as the bond formed during a romantic first kiss—or they can be negative hooks, such as the emotional wounds that are left following a breakup or a big blowout of a fight. These energetic hooks are electromagnetic connections between people through which thoughts, emotions, and energy continue to flow back and forth. You've probably experienced

> To love and be loved is to feel
> the sun from both sides.
>
> *Dr. David Viscott*

the power of energetic connections at some point in your life. Perhaps you finally decided to end a relationship, and you made a bold decision to move on emotionally. And then—surprise, surprise—suddenly your previous lover calls and wants you back. What happened? By making the decision to move on, you disrupted the energetic cord between you. At some unconscious level, your ex felt this and then reached out to you in order to reinstate the energetic connection.

To the extent you are connected in this way to any of your previous lovers, you will not be fully available to invest your energy in a new relationship. In addition, the remnants of negative energetic hooks can show up as actual physical pain. I have heard many cases where headaches, backaches, and all kinds of ailments have been resolved once these energetic cords have been cut.

So, how do we unhook these energetic cords? First, we must be very honest with ourselves and make sure we are really, truly emotionally ready to unhook. Once you are certain it's time to cut the cords, you can find an energy healer or do it yourself, using one of the techniques I'll share toward the end of this chapter.

Many years ago I read in a Native American book of lovers leaving "luminous cords of green light" in a woman's womb.

To release these energetic hooks, a woman would go into a cave for three days of meditation. There she would recall each of her past lovers, have an internal dialogue of forgiveness and appreciation with them, and when she was ready, she would envision herself physically cutting the cords that still connected them.

I didn't have a cave to go into, but as I was unhooking from past lovers in order to make space in my heart for my soulmate, I did spend time each day with a similar intention. I would begin by sitting quietly and meditating. I would then recall a past boyfriend or lover with whom I still felt energetically hooked. In my mind and heart I would thank him for having been in my life, for the ways he had been a catalyst for my growth, and for helping me to clarify the qualities I was really looking for in a man. With my eyes closed, I would have a dialogue with him, saying everything I felt needed to be said and sometimes even imagining what he might want to say to me. I would then imagine myself inside my womb, where an energetic cord still connected me to this past lover. In my mind's eye, I would find the cord that was attached to him and snip it with a small pair of scissors, watching it instantly disappear.

If that technique seems too strange (or if you are a man), you can imagine that the cords are connected to your second chakra, just south of your bellybutton. Close your eyes, see the cord that still links you to this person, have an internal dialogue where you say everything you need to say, then imagine taking a knife or a sharp pair of scissors and cutting the cord. Once it's cut, you may even be able to feel the energy you once projected onto that other person returning to you.

If you have a hard time with visualizations, you may prefer to do the following ritual, loosely adapted from the book *Your Hands Can Heal You* by Master Stephen Co and Eric B. Robins, M.D. The physicality of washing away your past and watching it go down the drain is very satisfying. You can even do it in combination with the technique I just described.

● ● ●

Items needed:

Ritual for Releasing the Past

❒ a 26-ounce container of salt (any kind of table salt but not Epsom salts)

❒ candles

❒ a large, clean bath towel

❒ fifteen to thirty minutes of uninterrupted time

Fill the bathtub with warm water and twenty-six ounces of salt. While the bathtub is filling up, light a few of your favorite candles and turn off the lights. Immerse your body in the salt water, and allow yourself to recall each of your previous lovers. As you think of each one, silently forgive him and ask him to forgive you for any ways in which you hurt each other. Thank him also for the positive things he brought to your life, the lessons you learned, and the clarity you now have as a result of having been with this person.

Then, imagine that there is an energetic cord that connects you to this person in a negative or limiting way. With your eyes closed, see if you can identify the place in your body where you still feel connected to this person; you might perceive it as longing, resentment, or even numbness. Breathe deeply and feel the ways that your connection to the past is making you unavailable for love in the present. Then visualize the cord that binds you to this person, and decide how you'd like to cut it. You can do it with a karate-chop motion or imitate holding a pair of scissors or a knife in your hand, snipping the cord between you. Once the cord is cut, clap your hands three times to dissipate and release the energy that once flowed through the energetic cord.

When you are finished, let the bath water drain, and then take a long shower (it is essential to cleanse yourself thoroughly after taking a salt bath). Using your favorite soap and shampoo, thoroughly cleanse your hair and body to eliminate all the salty water and with it any residue of negative energy that was once held in those energetic cords.

• • •

Sometimes we hold on to the past—even if it was painful or unfulfilling—as a way to distract ourselves from the depth of longing we have to find true love. In the throes of loneliness, we can easily become nostalgic or bitter about previous lovers, and without realizing it, we drain all our vitality from the present moment.

Think again about the man or woman you described in your Soulmate List. In order to establish a strong energetic connection with this person, you need to have all your resources focused in the here and now. To the extent that you're holding on to the past, you are not available to the present moment. This is a time to commit fully to the healing of your own heart, even if it means feeling the ache that your soulmate has not yet arrived. The desire you feel to connect with him or her is a potent magnetizer, and when your heart is open, you become approachable, unguarded, and utterly irresistible. Clearing the energetic hooks of your past sends a clear signal to the Universe that you are ready, willing, and able to merge with your soulmate right now.

CHAPTER SEVEN

taking
action

...

Find the person who will love you
because of your differences
and not in spite of them
and you have found a lover for life.

Leo Buscaglia

Many years ago I wrote the book *Hot Chocolate for the Mystical Lover: 101 True Stories of Soul Mates Brought Together by Divine Intervention*. Through the course of writing that book, I discovered some of the many ways soulmates find each other. It's pretty empowering to realize that even the most mystical, magical encounters required the soon-to-be lovers to take action—to deliberately put themselves in the "right place at the right time." Here are some of the things they did that really worked:

1. They set an intention and followed it up with action

After you've made your list of desired qualities and set the intention to find your perfect life partner, it's important that you be on the lookout for clues and prepare yourself mentally, emotionally, and physically when fate calls you to action. This was the winning formula that my friend Sean Roach, a successful CEO and speaker, used to find his soulmate.

At thirty-six, Sean was beginning to wonder if he'd ever find the right woman to settle down and start a family with. He traveled at least twice a week for work and had doubts that he'd be able to meet someone, given that he was hardly ever at home and spent only a day or two in each city. I shared with Sean some of the principles we've been exploring here, and although he had to admit he was not a firm believer in this "tree hugging stuff" (as he fondly referred to it), he decided to give it a try. He set an intention to find his perfect match, created a Treasure Map filled with images of happy couples lying in the sand and hanging out in the backyard by a firepit, and chose one image in particular—that of a man with a kid on his shoulders—to put on his iPod and cell phone where he could look at it daily.

One afternoon Sean was on a flight to Orlando to give a speech. Although he usually spent the whole flight working or catching up on e-mails, this time he happened to notice the flight attendant, Pia, who served him a glass of red wine. After a quick twenty-four-hour stay in Orlando, Sean boarded the plane back to the West Coast, only to discover that the same crew was working on his return flight. About an hour into the ride, Sean overheard a passenger speaking rudely to one of the attendants and was moved to take action. As he came to the flight attendant's defense, he found himself looking once again into Pia's eyes. Noticing the spark, one of the other flight attendants said, "Sean should get an award for intervening like that, and I think his reward should be Pia's number!" Sean did take down Pia's number and called her a week later. From the first dinner they shared, they felt as though they had known each other for years.

2. *They reunited with childhood or high-school sweethearts*

How many times have you had the thought, *I wonder whatever happened to so-and-so?* Many people find their true love by attending a reunion or as a result of hearing about a long-lost friend and then making the first move to reconnect. I recently read a story about a couple named Charlie and Carlyn Baily, both in their sixties, who married after finding each other on Classmates.com—forty-three years after graduating from high school. "It's still hard to believe," Carlyn said. "If this had been even ten years ago—no Classmates.com, no computers— it would have been literally pure accident to make contact." The fact is, today's technology makes this kind of reconnection easier than ever.

Sometimes reuniting with a past flame can spark business ideas as well. Consider the story of Jeff Tinley, who met his wife at their ten-year reunion and was so inspired by their reconnection that he founded Reunion.com!

3. *Some people (myself included) had dreams or premonitions that provided clues about how or where or when to find their soulmates, and they acted upon those clues*

> My great hope is to laugh
>
> as much as I cry;
>
> to get my work done
>
> and try to love somebody
>
> and have the courage
>
> to accept the love in return.
>
> *Maya Angelou*

One morning five years ago, Englishman David Brown woke up with a cellphone number running through his mind. Brown had no idea where the number came from, but he sent a text message to it anyway, hoping to solve the mystery. He reached Michelle Kitson, who lived sixty miles away. She had no explanation as to why her number would be running through his head, but after several messages back and forth, they ended up meeting and falling in love. David and Michelle were recently married and have just returned from their honeymoon in India. True stories like this are a clear reminder to listen to our dreams, trust our intuition, and have faith that the Universe is even now sending us signs that will lead us to love.

4. *Many had a "gut feeling" that they should go to specific places and made the choice to honor their intuition, even if they had other plans*

One woman, who was actually feeling quite depressed, had an impulse to go to an aquarium . . . someplace she had never been before and had no real desire to visit. But she went, and there she met the dolphin trainer, with whom she fell in love. They are now happily married and living in Hawaii. Another woman received a last-minute invitation to a party. She really didn't feel like socializing that night, but something inside her urged her to go. She met her husband at that party. More than a few were fixed up on blind dates by friends, and while they had never thought of themselves as the "blind date" type, they followed through anyway, only to discover that Cupid had struck.

5. They took action, joined an online dating service, and met their beloveds

I have more than one friend who met their husbands through an online dating service. In fact, I recently read an article that estimated 80 percent of the population will have an online virtual identity by the year 2011. And just in case you're thinking that a lack of Internet savvy will prevent you from taking advantage of the latest social-networking technology, think again! My eighty-year-old mother-in-law took action, with a little help from a younger, more computer-literate friend, and met the love of her life through Match.com.

6. They met their soulmates by taking the bold step to make adventure happen

I see a lot of people falling into the trap of postponing fun and adventure until *after* they meet their soulmates, reasoning that then they'll have someone to share the adventure with. I remember hearing the story of one man in particular who loved whales. He finally decided to take a kayak trip with a bunch of strangers so he could have the experience of seeing whales up close. Well, he not only saw the whales, he ended up meeting his soulmate who just happened to be kayaking right next to him. I know several couples who met on trips to foreign lands where they never expected to find romance. Vivian was from Boston; Mike was from Minneapolis. They met in Crete. Isn't love grand?

Sometimes the act of taking a bold step or following your heart's desire actually leads you to the doorstep of your beloved. For example, Gabrielle, a young woman I met in a marketing course I taught, had been passionate about learning Spanish since she was a teenager. She fantasized about meeting the perfect Latin lover who would patiently teach her to speak the language, then whisk her away for exotic vacations in Mexico. When she shared this, I urged her not to wait, but rather to follow her passion for learning the language. Who knew where it might lead? Sure enough, I heard from Gabrielle a couple of years later. She enrolled in a Spanish class at a local community college, and there she met a new friend who ended up introducing her to the man who is now her fiancé (and yes, he is Latin!).

• • •

The point of all these stories is that although you can't control the exact day, place, and time your soulmate will appear, you can increase your odds significantly by being actively involved in your own life. This often means pursuing interests that you've put on the back burner. Whatever you've been waiting for, this is the time to do it. If you love tennis but haven't picked up a racquet in years, join a tennis club or sign up for some lessons. If you daydream about taking nature hikes with your beloved, go on a guided tour at a nearby state park, or make it a point to stop by the beach or other recreational area after work. If you're an avid reader, join a book club.

Look at it this way: what's the worst that could happen if you decide to start actively pursuing your interests and passions? You'll probably end up making yourself happier, healthier, and more intellectually fit. You will also most likely end up meeting some interesting people, and you'll be broadcasting your unique tastes and preferences to the Universe even more clearly.

Now, does this mean you should fill every available hour in your appointment book with activities you hope will hasten the process of meeting your soulmate? Absolutely not! If you're driven to go out every night by the fear that your beloved will never find you if you stay home, you are missing the point. There is a huge difference between taking *inspired action* and taking *compulsive action*. Inspired action, as I'm defining it here, is when you already feel lovable and enjoy your own company and are then guided to do something that will amplify the joy you are already experiencing. Compulsive action, on the other hand, comes from a place of loneliness, desperation, and fear. Remember that the basic Law of Attraction states that "like attracts like." When your actions are driven from a place of emptiness or lack of fulfillment, it's quite possible you will only attract more of the same.

Trust that things will work out. Take action when the signs are there to take action, and don't feel pressured to act when the inspiration isn't there. As Peggy McColl, my dear friend and author of the New York Times bestseller *Your Destiny Switch*, discovered, sometimes love finds you when you make the choice to do nothing at all.

Peggy's Story
My Soulmate Came Knocking on My Door!

After my divorce, I was a stay-at-home mom running an Internet business, working in a home office with very little face-to-face contact with people. I lived in a residential neighborhood filled with families and, to my knowledge, not a single unattached man. Although I believed my soulmate was out there somewhere, it was hard not to notice the years ticking by as I waited for him to arrive. I also wondered *how* in the world he was going to find me, given that I worked from home and spent most of my days in semi-isolation.

Gradually, I let go of my need to know where or how he was going to come into my life, and one day early in January, I simply decided the following: *My soulmate and I are going to meet easily, effortlessly, and perfectly.* This, in fact, became my daily mantra, and I developed an unwavering emotion of faith.

One day shortly thereafter, I went for a walk with my dog, Noelle. After catching sight of another dog on the front lawn of a neighbor's house, Noelle bolted over to say "hello" to this new dog in the neighborhood. The moment the dog's owner walked out of the house, I thought, *Hmmm . . . he's handsome!* We started chatting, and in the middle of our conversation I found myself having another thought: *This is the kind of guy that I would like to be with.* He seemed gentle, kind, and caring, and he obviously liked dogs. Plus, he was handsome and masculine-looking. From that point on, I stayed open to the way that Mr. Right would show up in my life, resisting the urge to "make something happen" and having faith in the Universe, its timing, and its wisdom.

Then, one snowy winter morning, my doorbell rang, and there was my new neighbor asking me to take care of his dog because his doggy babysitter wasn't available and he was called into work (he was a pilot on call). After he returned from work, I invited him in for coffee, and the rest, as they say, is history. We fell in love and within a short period of time were an item. Two and a half years later we married.

A DAILY PRACTICE

Once you are living in the "knowing" that your soulmate is on the way, make it a daily practice to check in with your intuition about specific actions you can take to make your actual *meeting* a little easier.

Start each day with a prayer of gratitude and a reminder to yourself to turn your heart light on to high. As you come in contact with people throughout the day, smile at them and send them some love. Regardless of who you meet—man, woman, child, or beast—practice beaming love at them. You'll feel better and so will they, *and* you will be incredibly attractive while you are doing this.

✓ *Taking* this a step further, imagine that your soulmate is observing you 24/7, and use this perspective to evaluate the way you are behaving toward others. Are you being kind, loving, thoughtful, and attentive to those around you? Ask yourself what you would do differently if your soulmate were by your side, and conduct yourself in that manner starting today.

✓ *If,* after doing the exercises in this book, you have gotten clearer about what you are looking for in a partner, be sure to update your friends and let them know what is on your wish list.

✓ *Don't* be afraid to go to places alone. I know several women who met their beloveds at a coffee shop while they were sitting by themselves.

✓ *Change* your routine. Most of us are on automatic pilot much of the time, walking through our lives with blind-ers on and not even noticing what is right in front of us. Once a day, challenge yourself to do at least one thing differently. For example, for your fitness workout go to a new location or club, or if you are running or walking or biking, take a different route. Try a new yoga studio, or shop in a different grocery store (one of the coolest couples I know met in the bakery section at Costco). Why try new things? Because when you do, you are forced to pay more attention, to be more present. When you are more present (instead of being checked-out, multitask-ing, or lost in thought), you just might notice the one who is noticing you!

✓ *Pay* attention to synchronistic meetings and follow your intuitive hunches.

I recently sat down with Drew Heriot, who directed the film *The Secret*, and his fiancé, Jenny Keller. Drew and Jenny are an adorable couple who used the Law of Attraction, combining intuition with action, to manifest some pretty jaw-dropping results.

Drew and Jenny's Story
The Law of Attraction Works . . . Every Single Time

DREW: In 2006, I broke up with my girlfriend of four years. We both felt it would support our development as individuals to no longer be together.

JENNY: That was the year I moved out to Los Angeles from the Midwest. I was given the option to complete my externship for my doctorate anywhere I wanted, and I decided to take the opportunity to experience a new side to life, but with the reassurance of knowing I was only making a year-long commitment. How could I say no? However, only one month after moving, I broke up with my boyfriend of two years and realized that it was time to reevaluate what I wanted in my next relationship.

DREW: So, in October of 2006, unbeknownst to each other, Jenny and I were both lying on our beds—unaware of the other person's existence—writing down what we were each searching for in a partner. Well, I was writing. Jenn, in her usual fashion, was compiling a spreadsheet.

JENNY: Hey! I thought it was a great idea. I had my spreadsheet organized into columns of Must Haves, Would Like to Haves, and Will Not Tolerates.

DREW: After I clarified what I wanted in a woman, I sat back with the same eager expectation that I feel after ordering a delicious meal that I know is on its way. I surrendered the how, when, and where it would happen, and then the Universe, in classic style, created the most wonderful rendezvous with her about three months later. Jenny sat in front of me at a lecture given by John Demartini (one of the teachers featured in *The Secret*). His lecture was about—of all things—breaking through the myths and fantasies of relationship to create real intimacy.

JENNY: I almost didn't go that night. I came home from work that day and fell asleep on my bed, waking up with just enough time to throw some clothes on and head out the door. In my half-dazed state I seriously contemplated not going—arguing with myself that I was tired and I was just going alone so there was nobody to disappoint, but there was something inside of me telling me I needed to go. This feeling was no stranger to me; it was that inner voice that always says, *Something awaits.* So, when I heard it, I quickly got dressed and headed out the door.

The moment I walked into the room, I saw him. Actually we walked in together, and he sat behind me during the lecture. I remember thinking he was cute, and *Oh boy! He has an Australian accent. How did I forget to include that on my list?!*

DREW: She spun around in her seat for a quick chat. She was so beautiful and clear.

JENNY: After the lecture Drew went up to speak to John, and I got up to leave. But then I saw Drew and John talking, and I decided to muster up the courage to ask them if they would like to have coffee. So I bought one of John's books and headed up to the stage to ask him to sign it. I really didn't care about the signature—I just wanted to be closer to Drew.

DREW: Is that why you bought the book?

JENNY: Yes! I never told you?

DREW: Oh, sweetie, I didn't know that!

JENNY: Anyway, as I was getting John's autograph, Drew and I exchanged looks, but neither of us had the courage to ask the other one for a phone number.

DREW: I never did figure out how to ask for a phone number in a less than tacky way.

JENNY: At that moment, a couple of people walked up to Drew, and one said excitedly to the other, "And *this* is the director of *The Secret.*" Well, my immediate reaction took over. I left while Drew was in midsentence, giving a quick wave good-bye and deciding that the two of us lived in completely different worlds.

Ten days later my world led me to a wedding at Agape.

DREW: As did mine. Wow, we live in *such* different worlds, honey! When I saw you at that wedding, I started to get the message. After all, if I was the Universe trying to line me up with a girl, what better way than at a talk on intimate relationships and at a wedding?

JENNY (laughing): You left out the funniest part! When he sat down in the chair directly in front of me for the ceremony, I could hardly believe it. I kicked his chair, he spun around, shocked and obviously happy to see me, but the only thing that came out of his mouth was, "Oh dear, I didn't put any gel in the back of my hair."

DREW: Well, I didn't. It was quite embarrassing. The one time I don't and I have my lovely staring at the back of my head the whole night.

JENNY: We exchanged numbers that night.

DREW: Needless to say, she is everything on my list and so much more. And I found out later she had a list, too, and I'm everything on it.

JENNY: Beautiful, isn't it?

• • •

Of course, theirs *is* a beautiful story, but it's also one we can learn from. In order to manifest what we've told the Universe we want, we must remain alert to the inner stirrings of our intuition, but more importantly, we must be willing to follow up our hunches with action. Sometimes our intuition will guide us toward an action that is outside our familiar comfort zone. Jenny probably would have been more comfortable had she chosen to stay home and relax instead of going to the lecture that night—and if she had left rather than walking over to where Drew was standing. But summoning the courage to honor her instincts through action was what ultimately led her to her perfect partner.

There is an African proverb that says, "Pray with your feet moving." I take this to mean that manifestation is a balancing act between being and doing. When your intuition tells you it's time to relax, release the need to take action and just *be*. And when you're inspired to take action, go full out.

CHAPTER EIGHT

savor the waiting

...

I am bewildered by the magnificence
of your beauty, and wish to see you
with a hundred eyes. . . . I am in the house
of mercy, and my heart is a place of prayer.

Rumi

When the seeds of a flower have been planted in the ground and the first leaves begin to sprout, the gardener does not tug on the leaves every day to make the plant grow faster. He trusts that nature will play her role, and when the time is right, the flower will blossom. Like a gardener, you have planted a seed and invited love to unfold in your life. You have clarified the kind of person you want to be with; you have listened to your gut feelings; you have taken actions outside your typical comfort zone and have made space for your soulmate in your home and in your heart. Your work is done! You can now relax, enjoy, and trust that in time, with steady nourishment and attention, those seeds will blossom and bear fruit. Your only intention at this point is to find pleasure in the journey itself and savor the experience of joyfully anticipating your soulmate's arrival.

Around the same time that I was writing this book, Brian and I were preparing to take a special vacation to French Polynesia to celebrate his fiftieth birthday. We booked the trip months in advance, so we had plenty of time to plan our itinerary, think about which sights we wanted to see, and generate a great deal of excitement about what was to come. Of course, spending ten days in paradise was wonderful, but I have to say that the process of preparing for the trip was equally enjoyable. In fact, as I shopped, packed, and read about the history and geography of the islands, I actually felt like my vacation had already begun. The end result—actually being away together in a lush, tropical setting for ten days—was very fulfilling, but so was the process of getting there. In the days and weeks leading up to the trip, as I thought of another item to bring or went about handling the business that needed to be attended to while I was away, I savored the moments leading up to our actual journey, knowing that all my efforts would culminate in a long-awaited reward. This is what it means to "savor the waiting."

Let me give you another example. My friend Claudia loves to cook delicious meals for her family and friends, but it's not the act of putting the food on the table—or even watching her guests enjoy the delicious meal she has prepared—that she finds the most enjoyable. As she explained to me recently, she loves the scheming, the planning, the process of coming up with new recipes and new combinations of her favorite foods to share with others. She looks forward to the experience of shopping at specialty food stores to select the perfect fresh ingredients for each meal. She daydreams about the wine, the seating arrangements, and the special ambiance she wants to create for each occasion. She loves to put on music, stir the pot, and enjoy the aromas that fill her home as she cooks. She prides herself on selecting the perfect type of food for each circle of friends—South American cuisine for her friend Carolina, who is from Chile; Thai for her friends Nancy and Jane, who love spicy food. Claudia went so far as to say she actually thrives on being ultraefficient at work on the days when she is hosting a dinner party. For Claudia, the whole experience of preparing the meal is every bit as enjoyable as the act of consuming it—maybe even more so.

In this same spirit, I invite you now to savor the experience of magnetizing your perfect lover into your life. Celebrate the fact that you have been inspired to greater clarity about the kind of relationship you want. Welcome the feeling of your heart being more open than it has been in the past. Allow the new space in your home and in your life to inspire you, to give you motivation, and to propel you in a positive direction.

Every time you imagine what your soulmate will be like, and every time you fantasize about the day you'll meet, you get to choose between two distinct states of being. You can choose to linger in the longing, the aching, the wanting, and the waiting, or you can consciously choose to bask in a state of joyful antic- ipation and excitement. Through the quality of your thoughts and feelings, you create the emotional tone of this time in your life. Every possibility is available to you. On one end of the spectrum, you can allow yourself to feel desperate and alone;

on the other end, you can feel ecstatic and blessed. There are multiple ways of perceiving every experience—riding a rollercoaster, for example—and your perception of your current circumstances will inform your overall emotional state. You can choose to be terrified as the rollercoaster makes its way slowly up to the top and create the experience of stress and anxiety as you imagine what's to come. Or you can throw your hands in the air and say to yourself, *This is where I am right now. This is the experience life is offering me. I may as well enjoy the ride!*

Having offered you this basic choice, I also want you to know that I definitely understand how difficult it can be when you truly feel ready to share your life with someone and he or she has not yet arrived. Special occasions like weddings, dinner parties, family gatherings, and holidays can be especially rough, so it's vital that you set yourself up in the right frame of mind before the event.

I once read a story about a woman who, when gearing up for another holiday season without a partner, decided to do something really creative. She took herself through a meditative process where she envisioned herself with her husband, having already been married for several years. She imagined them reminiscing about their lives before they met each other. Then she asked herself what I think is a remarkable question: *What kind of stories and experiences from my past do I look forward to one day sharing with him?* This question opened her up to a

perspective that she had never before considered, and a flood of creative ideas suddenly started coming
to her. From this new vantage point
she saw that she wanted her soulmate to understand the depth of
her caring and generosity toward
people. This insight gave her the
inspiration to organize a clothing

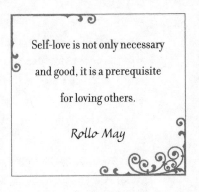

Self-love is not only necessary
and good, it is a prerequisite
for loving others.

Rollo May

drive for a local organization that helps single mothers. She
also realized she wanted her soulmate to appreciate her sense
of fun and adventure. This insight gave her the inspiration to
schedule an impromptu day cruise with a couple of girlfriends.
Finally, she saw that she wanted her soulmate to know that she
was a woman who values her sensuality and loves to be pam-
pered. This insight gave her the inspiration to cash in a gift
card to a spa that she'd had for several months and to devote
an entire day to pampering herself, complete with exercise,
steam, a pedicure, and a facial.

What she did next was really brilliant. She decided to cap-
ture "Christmas 1997" by taking photos of every occasion, so
she put together a scrap book titled, "What I Did the Christmas
when I Was Waiting for You." She got very creative with this
scrapbook, filling it not only with pictures but with little "did
you know?" facts about herself that she thought her soulmate
might find adorable and amusing: she had been a baton twirler

when she was in high school; when she was ten, she organized a neighborhood mission to find homes for stray dogs and cats; when she was twelve, she had a huge crush on Elton John. As she made the most of the holidays and added each picture and story to her scrapbook, she suddenly felt as though her soulmate was watching her from the future (which, as it turns out, he was). As a result, she planned her activities more deliberately and savored them more completely. Even though she did not meet her soulmate until the summer of 1998, she insists that they had spent the previous holiday season together.

If you knew without a shadow of doubt that your first date with the man or woman of your dreams was just months away, what would you do now to ensure that you make the most of this time? I designed the next feelingization to allow you to see your life right now through the eyes of the partnership you will one day create.

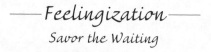

Feelingization
Savor the Waiting

Find a quiet, soothing place in your home to sit and relax. Place your body in a comfortable position and begin by taking a few deep breaths. Feel yourself melt into your seat as you begin to unwind, allowing any stress or tension to drain out of you and into the floor beneath your feet.

As you relax, allow your attention to scan your whole body, and notice the places within you that feel warm, mellow, and at ease. Breathe into those mellow spaces, allowing them to spread and expand out, encompassing your entire body.

On your next breath, I want you to imagine that it's five years from now and you are with your beloved in a nice, quiet space, just like you're in now. Maybe you're sitting together at a candlelit table for two; maybe you're snuggling together in bed. Take a moment to fill in the details that only your heart can provide about where you are and what you're doing. Are you married? Do you have children? Breathe in and allow yourself to feel the joy of this scene. Your dream has come true. You are with your soulmate, and you are blissfully in love. Allow this reality to penetrate deeply into every fiber of your heart and mind.

Imagine looking into your beloved's eyes and reminiscing about what you were doing just before you met. What aspects of your single life are you most proud to share? How did you enjoy yourself and savor each day as you prepared your life and your heart for his or her arrival? From the vantage point of now being deeply connected with your soulmate, reflect back on the things you did before you met that made you happy, proud, and radiant.

Notice how good it feels to know that you were in a place of feeling great about yourself—even before you met your partner. Long before your soulmate fell in love with you, you were in love with yourself and your life—making the most out of every day and bringing forth the best of yourself wherever you went. Notice how good that feels and breathe it in. You might experience it as a happy feeling or as a sense of pride and accomplishment, or maybe it's a more sensual, "ooooh . . . that's nice!" kind of feeling. As you allow this feeling to grow stronger, notice that it's starting to take on a particular color and shape, like a beautiful bubble that is surrounding your entire body. Notice what color your bubble of joyful anticipation is and allow it to surround and enter your heart, beam out through your eyes, and radiate from every part of your body. From across time and distance, you and your perfect soulmate are connected even at this moment, and every time you experience joy, happiness, and fun, this bubble of joy shines like a lighthouse that guides him or her home to you. Every day matters. Every choice matters. And it's up to you to make the most of your life right now.

Now bring your attention back into this present moment, carrying this joyful feeling with you. Know that as you commit to making the most of every day, you are joining in consciousness with your beloved. As you are preparing yourself for his arrival, he is preparing himself for yours. Breathe in deeply and savor the waiting, knowing that your destiny is in the hands of the Universe and your beloved is on the way.

Take one last long, deep breath, and as you breathe out, place your hands together in a prayer position over your heart as a way to anchor yourself in the memory and feeling of joyful anticipation.

Then, when you are ready, slowly open your eyes.

• • •

After completing this feelingization, take a moment to journal about the kinds of things you look forward to reminiscing about with your soulmate, and make a commitment to create those experiences for yourself now. Chances are, those particular ideas came to you for a reason, and following through with them will be rewarding in ways that you cannot even begin to imagine.

A LOVE LETTER FROM GOD

I received a copy of the following letter more than twenty years ago and have never been able to find out who originally wrote it. When I was single, reading this letter was very inspiring, which is why I am sharing it with you now. As you read it (and I recommend you do this daily), breathe in the truth of these words, and notice if they open up any more space inside of you to enjoy what you have in the present, even as you joyfully anticipate what the future holds.

Dear One,
Everyone longs to give themselves completely to someone, to have a deep soul relationship with another, to be loved thoroughly and exclusively, but I say "No." Not until you are satisfied, fulfilled and content with being alone, with giving yourself totally and unreservedly to Me, will you be ready to have the intensely personal and unique relationship that I have planned for you. You will never be united with anyone or anything else

until you are united with Me. I want you to stop planning, stop wishing, and start allowing Me to give you the most thrilling plan in existence—one that you cannot even imagine. I want you to have the best. Please, allow Me to bring it to you.

You must keep watching Me expecting the greatest of things. Keep experiencing the satisfaction that I AM. Keep listening and learning the things that I will tell you. Just wait. That's all. Don't be anxious. Don't worry. Don't look around at the things others have or that I have given them. Don't look at the things you think you want. Just keep looking up to Me or you will miss what I want to show you. And then, when you are ready, I will surprise you with a love far more wonderful than any you have dreamed of.

You see, until you are ready and until the one I have for you is ready (I am working even at this moment to have you both ready at the same time), until you are both satisfied exclusively with Me and the life I have prepared for you, you won't be able to experience the love that exemplifies your relationship with Me. This is Perfect Love.

And Dear One, I want you to have this most wonderful love. I want to see in the flesh a picture of your relationship with Me, and to enjoy materially and concretely the everlasting union of beauty, perfection, and love that I offer. Know that I love you utterly. Believe it and be satisfied.

Love,
God

CHAPTER NINE

falling
in love
with yourself

...

*You, yourself, as much as anybody
in the entire Universe, deserve
your love and affection.*

Buddha

andhi once said that we must "become the change we wish to see in the world." As you prepare to manifest your soulmate, you can apply this timeless wisdom to your own life by *becoming* the lover, the friend, the playmate, the partner, and the soulmate you have been looking for.

Think about that for a moment. We spend so much time and energy projecting into the future about how great we'll feel, how well we'll care for ourselves, and how proud we'll be once we finally meet our soulmate. This kind of thinking may leave us feeling excited about the future, but it does nothing for us in the present. While it's sometimes true that meeting someone—a lover, a friend, or even a boss or colleague—is the catalyst that inspires us to grow in a positive direction, more often than not, it works in the reverse. *First* we decide to grow, to love ourselves, to make the best of who we are and where we are in our lives, and *then* our commitment draws opportunities for love and connection out of the woodwork and into our lives.

As you reflect on the qualities you are looking for in a soul-mate, you must ask yourself whether you are demonstrating those qualities in your own life, and if not, what you would need to do to cultivate them. Just as a seed grows with the warmth of the sun, so our positive qualities grow when we put our attention on them.

Let me give you an example: if your wish is to be with some-one who is affectionate, devoted, and kind, you need to make the commitment to bring forth those qualities in yourself. Look for every opportunity to demonstrate devotion, kindness, and affection to the world around you—whether it's with the store clerk, the mail carrier, the telemarketer (I know, that's a tough one) . . . or, most importantly, with *yourself*! If you are seek-ing a man or a woman who is passionate, generous, and outgo-ing, you should be spending every minute of every day looking for ways to feed, nurture, and develop those facets of yourself. Not in the future, but in your life as it exists at this moment. A great way to think of this assignment is to imagine that you are the man or woman of your dreams and then to ask yourself, *If I were my beloved, would I fall in love with me?* If the answer is no, then dedicate yourself to becoming someone you would fall in love with. Remember the old saying "Laugh and the world laughs with you"? It's also true that when you fall in love with yourself, the whole world mirrors that love back to you. The following exercise will help you clarify the steps you need to take in order to *become* the love you've been seeking.

• • •

What you will need:

❐ several sheets of paper and a pen

❐ a comfortable chair

❐ fifteen to thirty minutes of uninterrupted time

Imagine you are writing an online ad and need to list your top ten assets, then take a moment to list your most lovable traits. If you get stuck, just think about the things other people compliment you for. Are you generous, compassionate, friendly, kind, considerate, thoughtful, interesting, or funny? Write them down.

As you read over this list, make sure it reflects the very best of you. If it doesn't, rework it until it does. No one else will ever need to see this list—it's just for you, so please don't hold back.

Once you have a list of your ten most luscious, desirable, and admirable qualities, it's time to create a daily affirmation that incorporates these truths about yourself. It might look like this: I am a passionate, compassionate, loving, friendly, helpful, adventurous, nurturing, sensual, spiritually connected woman, and I love all of me, *all of the time.*

Twice a day for the next thirty days, I want you to stand in front of a mirror with a big smile on your face, and speak your affirmation out loud. Be sure to look into your own eyes while speaking the truth about yourself. And just so you know, this might feel very, very awkward at first. Do it anyway.

This is a time to find the inner motivation to bring out the very best in yourself—not for the sake of your soulmate but for the sake of your own happiness and fulfillment. When you can do that, you will have discovered one of the most powerful keys to drawing to yourself virtually everything you desire. And if the idea of falling in love with yourself sounds selfish or self-absorbed, let me assure you, it's not. Look at it this way: If you're not in love with yourself; if you don't have an honest and gut-level appreciation of the adorable, juicy, one-of-a-kind characteristics that only you possess; if you haven't yet found compassionate acceptance for your flaws and discovered the ways they have made you uniquely who you are; if you don't approach your body with tenderness and sensuality; how can you expect your soulmate to do these things? The simple truth is that when you love yourself, you become absolutely irresistible.

The whole notion of self-love is talked about a lot these days, but I'd like to break it down into practical terms. The last time you flew on an airplane, you may have heard the flight attendant explain that in the event of a change in cabin pressure, you must secure your own oxygen mask before trying to help others with theirs. This is because when a plane is losing cabin pressure, you only have about six seconds before you lose consciousness, and if you don't use that time to put your own mask on, you will not be in any position to help someone else.

This example speaks volumes about self-love. If you aren't nourishing yourself on all levels with love, appreciation, healthy food, positive thoughts, and tenderness, you simply won't have the inner resources to love and nourish another. Loving yourself means being as attentive to your own needs as you are to the needs of your lover. It means caring for yourself as if you're the most important person in the world. It demands that you take the time to explore and discover what's really important to you—in life and definitely in love. When you truly love yourself, you are no longer willing to compromise your standards, because you value your happiness too much. Applying this single principle was the key that unlocked the soulmate mystery for my friend and marketing whiz Stefanie Hartman.

Stefanie's Story
A Perfect Fit

(Continued from chapter 1)

OK. I'll admit it right off the top. I was one of those girls who, while I romanced the idea of a perfect soulmate, deep down thought it was all hooey. Nonetheless, my mother had always told me, "Don't look down or behind you; just look ahead, and happiness will find you." And it did—as soon as I stopped chasing it.

So how'd I manifest my perfect fit?

To make a long story short, I became determined not to date any more men who were "almosts"—even the ones who were 99 percent almosts. I made the decision to give up Mr. Potential (they never reach it—trust me) in order to find Mr. Right.

At one point, I announced to my friends out loud that I am a good person, I really like who I am, and I'm just not willing to compromise anymore. I went so far as to make a list of qualities I must have in a man, as well as those I would not tolerate—all of which were based on knowing myself first. I knew I had love to give, but I no longer had a void to fill. There is a *big* difference, by the way. If a guy isn't right from the start, he's not worth my time. I didn't want any more fixer-uppers. I got to the place where I said, "That's it! Forget all this soulmate searching. I am hanging out with my girlfriends, doing yoga, having fun, and going for walks in the sun by myself." In other words, I started to connect with *me* again.

Well, about a week after I made that statement, my best friend called with the notion of sending me on a blind date with a man named Jarrod. I protested. Was she kidding? Did she not hear my vow? She said it would be a fun, "safe" date (I'm still not sure what that meant). In fact, she said, she dated him herself once months ago. "Great," I said, sarcastically. "Leftovers—why didn't you just open with that?"

I now joke that my best friend actually prescreened my husband before our first date. She explained that she met Jarrod over the Internet and went on a date with him almost a year before, but there was no chemistry, no spark. At the same time, this friend of mine met another guy—one she ended up marrying two weeks before my wedding. So in the same weekend she actually met my husband and hers. She's very organized.

An introduction was made via e-mail, and we began to chat back and forth for a couple of weeks. Then we graduated to a live phone call, and then we decided to meet in person. I was at a disadvantage, because my friend had sent him to my website, so he knew what I did and how I looked, and he had even read my "ten things you may not want to know about Stefanie" list, while I knew *nothing* about him. He even joked he had bad skin and still lived with his mother just to worry me further. I suggested dinner on Saturday, but he suggested we meet for coffee first (Mr. Bachelor had had too many bad first dates and didn't want to "waste" a Saturday night). If that went well, he explained, he might make an offer to proceed on to a dinner. I had no idea I had an ego before that moment. I had just been insulted by what I considered to be a "dating downgrade." (Obviously he had no idea that there were many men just waiting on the Internet to date me . . . hmph!) As it turned out, his comment upset me just enough to make me curious to find out who this guy was.

In girly revenge I got back at him by changing out of my newly purchased cute "date outfit" into jeans and tank top and beach sandals. I couldn't think of any outfit that said "I couldn't care less" any better. Satisfied at my own wittiness,

I waited for his arrival. Then a knock came and I opened the door.

We stared at each other in silence as the door swung open. He was thinking, *Wow she's hot . . . jackpot!* (his words, not mine—damn tank top, I was so not thinking like a man), and I was thinking, *Oh no, I wore the wrong outfit,* seeing as he was all dressed up and looked incredible. Suffice to say we made it past coffee, and in fact our first date lasted eight hours. Between coffee and dinner, I did make him wait while I did a quick "costume change" to my originally planned outfit, which was worthy of a great date.

So this is where our "serial monogamist" meets . . . "the juggler," let's call him (there are other names, but this seems the most pleasant). He was certainly enjoying the single life. While our dating styles differed, we both were determined not to settle or get serious with an "almost" (he, too, had experienced a painful break-up), and while I wrote my list of what I wanted in a partner, he had a mental one—his was more of a "feeling," which he thought he would just know when he met her.

After our second date, Mr. Bachelor (juggling five girls in two countries) told his best friend—in their postdate debrief—that he had met the woman he was going to marry. He actually said, "It was as if fate had delivered me my perfect woman, and I just recognized her. I knew my life was about to change; I just knew this was the woman I would spend my life with." His friends couldn't believe what was coming out of his mouth, because it was so unlike him. Obviously that night he had a few difficult phone calls to make. Sorry, girls!

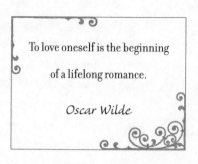

To love oneself is the beginning of a lifelong romance.

Oscar Wilde

We were engaged, bought a house, adopted a dog, and got married all within two years to the day we met. Nothing felt rushed; everything felt right. Marriage seemed so inevitable, so natural, and so right from early on in our dating. One of my favorite moments of that very special wedding day was the way I made Jarrod smile and laugh to the point where he began to tear up during the ceremony (he'll tell you he had something in his eye). I was unexpectedly so calm, so ready to walk down the aisle, that I almost sprinted—my dad had to hold me back.

We have never been afraid of being real with each other; in fact we both demanded it from the start. This was highlighted during our very serious vows ceremony. Jarrod had been "advised" by married men that as soon as we were married, his opinion would never matter again. We wrote our own vows, and when I said, "I promise to listen to you when you speak," I didn't even finish the sentence before Jarrod started to crack up. He couldn't stop laughing. So I held up the written-out vows and said, "I will! It's written here in black and white!" and then the whole room was in stitches. Who said a wedding ceremony has to be boring?

Meeting Jarrod made me realize that the way you recognize a true soulmate is that his character—his deepest and most treasured value system—matches your own. If I could tell you one thing to look for in a soulmate, it would be the feeling of recognition that conveys the sense of "I'm home."

When I met Jarrod, we instantly felt we had known each other before, as if we already had history. We felt very peaceful, very much ourselves, like we'd found our home in each other—and for a girl who travels as much as I do, this was a magical experience.

I now believe there really is a perfect soulmate for everyone. As soon as you stop trying to make the "almosts" fit, you'll find that the perfect match is out there just waiting for you.

• • •

Manifesting your soulmate using the Law of Attraction is not a numbers game! It's a very personal request that you are making of the Universe to bring you the love that your heart deserves and desires. Upholding your standards and values—even if it means giving up the instant gratification of dating someone charming but who you know isn't right for you—is the essence of self-love. And loving ourselves is an essential prerequisite to allowing others to love us.

To support you in falling more deeply in love with yourself, my sister, Debbie Ford, contributed the final feelingization. I recommend that you download this feelingization at www.soulmatesecret.com/audio and listen to it at least once a day, preferably at night before drifting off to sleep.

—Feelingization—
Loving Yourself

When I can love all of me, then I am able to love all of you. Approach this exercise with the intention of falling in love with your most magnificent self: your worthy, loving, and wholly unique self.

Inhale and exhale deeply, and with each exhale allow yourself to go deeper and deeper inside, to that very quiet and still place where all the wisdom and all the courage and all the love that you need reside. Imagine you're just floating into that very quiet, safe place with the intent to fall completely and madly in love with you.

Now take another deep breath, and on the exhale, imagine you're floating into this loveseat, a place where you feel cozy and comfortable and nourished.

I want you to now look off to your left, where you are going to see an image of you. It's an image of your most lovable self: the part of you that radiates joy and hope; the part of you that knows you are special and unique and that there's nobody in the world like you.

What does that aspect of you look like? Maybe you'll see an image of yourself when you were two or three or seven or fifteen or twenty-two. It's you when you're radiating love. Your eyes are lit up. You are irresistible.

And just invite that aspect to come and sit before you, taking one more slow, deep breath and allowing that exhale to connect you heart-to-heart with this part of yourself. And ask this aspect of you to tell you what's great about you. What makes you so special, so warm, so wonderful?

Allow yourself to hear from your most lovable self all the reasons why you are worthy and deserving of meeting and enjoying the love of your life. Allow yourself to hear all the reasons why you should fall madly and passionately in love with you. Ask that part of you to show you the good you've done and the people you've supported whose lives have been enriched because of you.

Allow yourself to hear the qualities you possess that make you unique, that are important, that make you so lovable.

Now ask your most lovable self what you would need to give up in order to fall madly in love with yourself again and again and again. What thoughts would you have to give up? What beliefs would you have to let go of? What behaviors or patterns do you need to leave behind in order for you to feel how special, how desirable, how awesome you are?

Just breathe in and exhale, allowing yourself to hear what you just heard. And if you're willing to give that up in the name of love, just acknowledge that to this part of you, and see what you could do this week to ensure that you'll give that up. Is there a structure you need to put in place, someone you need to call, somebody's support you need to enlist?

And if you're willing to do that, just acknowledge that to yourself and to this lovable aspect, this part of you.

And now ask this part of you to tell you the sweet words that you need to say to yourself each and every day to feel loved, to feel loving, to feel lovable. What sweet words do you need to hear to be in the presence of love each and every day? Is it that you are kind, that you're perfect as you are, that you are sexy, beautiful, brilliant, and wonderful? Is it that you're a genius? Is it that you're worthy? Is it that you're desirable? Is it that you're competent, creative, special, important?

Take a deep breath, and breathe in those words. Say them to yourself now seven times.

Allow yourself to see those words being etched across your consciousness. Just breathe them in, because you are so worthy of love.

Notice how your heart is softening. Notice how those words make you feel appreciated. Those are your words. You heard them from the most lovable part of you.

So acknowledge the magnificence of your humanity. Acknowledge the goodness of your heart.

And just take another slow, deep breath, allowing that exhale to melt away anything between you and being one with love. Allow yourself to see how your loving yourself would benefit the people in your life: your children, your siblings, your co-workers, the people in your community, your friends. Really see that to love yourself completely is to give love to each and every person you meet. Allow yourself to see that now.

And now imagine all the people in your life—all the people you love and those who love you—coming and kissing you on the cheek, the people who are still here and the people who are gone. Allow yourself to hear them cheering you on, and allow their love to penetrate every cell in your body.

And then on your next exhale, just repeat these words:

"I am loved. I am lovable. I am love."

"I am loved. I am lovable. I am love."

"I am loved. I am lovable. I am love."

Allow anything that's between you and those words to melt off of you to the floor beneath your feet. And just repeat this mantra seven times, allowing the vibration of those words to melt away anything that exists between you and that reality.

"I am loved. I am lovable. I *am* love."

And so it is.

• • •

All there is for you to do at this point is to continue being the wonderful person you are and continue falling more passionately in love with yourself each day. Tend to the space you've created, be responsive to new opportunities, live in the knowingness that you are in a loving, committed relationship, and savor the waiting for your beloved to arrive.

CHAPTER TEN

are you ready for BIG LOVE?

...

Where there is great love,
there are always miracles.

Willa Cather

A re you really ready for BIG LOVE? If you can respond with a resounding *Yes* to each of these statements, you are indeed ready:

I believe I am deserving of BIG LOVE and that The One is out there and he/she is also looking for me._____

I am clear about the nature of the person and relationship I now wish to manifest._____

I have healed the baggage of my past relationships._____

I have created a Treasure Map, prepared the relationship corner of my home and bedroom, and have written and released my Soulmate List to the Universe._____

I love myself and sincerely enjoy the pleasure of my own company._____

I have the time, energy, and resources to nurture another.____

I'm living as if my soulmate were already with me, while I savor the waiting for his/her arrival._____

If you responded yes to these statements, congratulations! By applying the principles and working through the exercises outlined in this book, you have done your part to magnetize your soulmate into your life. You have clarified exactly what you want in a soulmate, and you have "placed your order" with the Universe. You have tended to the emotional wounds that may have unwittingly kept love away. You've cleared out the clutter in your life, your heart, and your home in joyful anticipation of your soulmate's arrival. You've created space for new love to grow. You've rearranged your beliefs so that you are even now drawing to yourself the loving, committed relationship that you desire and deserve. And perhaps most important of all, you have learned that who you are *being* is a far more power-ful attractor than anything you can *do.* In other words, you are having a full-blown love affair with yourself.

I vividly remember this period in my own life as being a very fertile and productive time. You see, as you fall in love with yourself, you don't just attract more love. You attract more friendships, more opportunities, more success—more of ev-erything that you desire. I also remember the day I came to a startling realization: *Even if I never met my soulmate, I had—and would continue to have—a great life.* This may sound like a para-dox, but the moment I could embrace both feelings at once—

the feeling of loving my life exactly as it was and the feeling of wanting to share it with another—I was suddenly at peace. It was not long after coming to this realization that I had a magical encounter with a holy woman that changed my life forever.

On June 22, 1997, I went to see Amma, the hugging saint from India. I had heard about her years earlier from Deepak Chopra, who said to me: "Amma is the real thing. If you ever have a chance to get a hug from her, do it." I signed up to attend a weekend retreat, knowing that during this retreat I would receive at least two hugs. I had spent the previous year forgiving myself and others for relationships that hadn't worked out, I had made my Soulmate List and released it to the Universe, I had unhooked myself energetically from past lovers, and I truly believed in my heart that my soulmate was out there. Now I was hoping for a little cosmic power boost to help bring us together.

On the first evening of the retreat, I patiently waited in line for my hug. I was excited and a little nervous . . . I had a plan but I didn't know if it would work. I had been told that when you receive a hug from Amma, she may whisper or chant into your ear but you don't converse with her, because she doesn't speak English. Finally it was my turn, and while she was hugging me, I whispered in her ear, "Dear Amma, please heal my heart of anything that is stopping me from finding my soulmate." She laughed as I said this and squeezed me tighter. I "knew" that she had understood my prayer.

That night I had a very vivid dream. In the dream there were seven women dressed in purple, singing to me. The lyrics of the song were: "Arielle is the woman that comes after Beth." When I woke up in the morning, I was convinced it had been a sign—my soulmate was out there, but he was currently with someone named Beth.

The next evening I had an opportunity for a second hug from Amma. This time I whispered in her ear to please send me my soulmate, and I rattled off part of my wish list. Again she laughed and squeezed me tight.

Three weeks later I went on an unexpected business trip to Portland, Oregon. One of the authors I had been working with, Nick, was about to be interviewed for an important TV show. The taping had been moved from the studio in L.A. to Nick's home in Portland, and the publisher asked me to fly up and supervise the shoot. The call came late in the afternoon on a Thursday, and I needed to be in Portland the following morning. I called Nick's office and spoke to one of his business associates, Brian, who agreed to pick me up at the airport the following day. He kindly explained to me that because the Portland airport was under construction, he couldn't meet me at the gate, but he did tell me where I could find him just outside the terminal.

On the flight up to Portland, I was unusually nervous. At first I thought it was because I was in the middle of a detox diet—I had been subsisting on various juice and soup concoctions for about a week. However, I would find out soon enough where my "nerves" were coming from. When I landed at the gate, I followed Brian's directions out of the terminal and quickly found him. The moment I saw him, I had the thought, *I wonder who Beth is?* This was quickly followed by the thought, *He's not your type and you are a little crazy today*.

> Life has taught us that love does not consist in gazing at each other but in looking outward together in the same direction.
>
> *Antoine de Saint-Exupery*

When we arrived at Nick's house, the TV crew was setting up for the interview. When they were ready to begin taping, I sat in the back of the room on a little bench next to Brian. I should have been concentrating on the conversation between Nick and the host of the show, but I kept getting distracted by an overwhelming urge to massage Brian's shoulders. The urge was so intense that I literally had to sit on my hands so I wouldn't be tempted! As I was sitting on that bench next to Brian, whom I had met only an hour earlier, I very clearly heard a voice say to me, *He's The One. This is how it happens. This is who you are going to spend your life with*.

By now I was convinced that I was losing my mind. I had never heard voices before, nor had I ever been compelled to rub a stranger's shoulders. What was going on? When the interview was complete, the lights went on and we stood up. Brian turned to me and asked, "When I picked you up at the airport, did I look familiar to you?" Slightly taken aback, I answered, "Yes, why do you ask?" And he said, "Because I've been dreaming about you."

I was so blown away by what he said that I just turned and began walking to the door to get some fresh air. As I was walking away, I heard Nick say to Brian, "Let's take Arielle to dinner tonight before she has to catch her plane, and why don't you invite Elizabeth to join us?" As I reached the lakeside patio to sit down, I thought, *Great. So there* is *a Beth. Not only a Beth, but an* Elizabeth. *It must be his wife.* Then the voice came back and said simply, *Don't worry. They are just like brother and sister.*

I didn't know what any of this meant. I was excited, hungry, and more than a bit confused. Later that day Brian and I went to dinner with Nick, his wife, a few other people—and Elizabeth, who arrived with a friend. It was a hot summer evening, and the restaurant service couldn't have been slower. We ordered our dinner, but it was taking forever to arrive. Before our meal was even served, it was time for me to go because I had to catch my flight home. Nick arranged for my trout dinner to be put into a to-go box, and Brian raced down the freeway to get me to the airport on time. As we were driving, I was feeding both of us my trout dinner and hearing myself say things I couldn't believe were coming out of my mouth. Things like, "You know, I don't want to have any children." To which Brian responded, "That's why Elizabeth and I have broken up. She wants to get married and have children, and I don't want to."

Then I heard myself say, "I've been looking for a tantra partner." At that point Brian nearly drove off the road. (I later found out that he *had* been dreaming about me for the past three weeks, and the night before he picked me up at the airport, we were in the tantric yab-yum position. This is when a man is sitting cross-legged and a woman sits on top of him and wraps her legs around his back and they are in full union, all chakras connected.)

We arrived at the airport. After a quick hug goodbye, I ran to catch my plane. As I waited in the terminal, I put in a call to my Vedic astrologer, Marc Boney. I briefly told him about Brian and gave him his birth info (which I had managed to extract from Brian before I caught my plane). By the time I got home, Marc had left a voice message for me that said: "I looked up both of your charts. This is the clearest indication of a fated relationship I have ever seen. I predict you will marry him."

One week later both Nick and Brian came to San Diego for Nick's book tour. Brian and I sat in the back of the room while Nick gave his lecture, writing notes to each other like seventh graders! Things moved very quickly from there. Brian and I became engaged three weeks later. Within two months he moved to La Jolla to live with me. Exactly one year to the date that I asked Amma to help me find my soulmate (which was the culmination of two years of deliberately applying the Soulmate Secrets you have just learned), she married us in a Hindu ceremony in front of thousands of people.

I know with certainty that the preparation I did prior to meeting Brian is the reason we are together today. I needed to experience "bad" love before I was ready for BIG LOVE. I needed to marry myself first and grow into the loving, spiritual, happy, successful being that I am, because only then would I be an energetic match for my soulmate. The same held true for Brian. There was work he had to do, clarity he had to attain, and relationships he needed to resolve before he was ready to share his life with me.

I want to suggest that this is also true for you and your beloved. Think of it like a great production—a Broadway play, for example. The brilliance and beauty of opening night was created layer upon layer in the all-important period leading up to the opening. It may seem like magic to the audience, but countless hours of deliberate intent have gone on behind the scenes. So as you set the stage for your great love story, as you rewrite the script, refine the plot, and assemble the perfect cast, know that the relationship you will enjoy with your beloved will reflect back to you the love, care, and attention you have given it along the way.

And know, too, that even as you methodically implement the principles and exercises you've learned here, you can never claim complete ownership of, nor 100 percent control over, the process. There is always an unseen force that is guiding your hand, nudging you along in the form of inspiration, and taking great pleasure in every step of the process as it unfolds.

As human beings, we have free will over our own choices, thoughts, beliefs, and actions. And as universal beings who are part of a greater whole, we are carried along in the current of divine timing. Where each of these forces intersects is what some call magic.

Prepare yourself, surrender the timing, and enjoy the ride.

Sending you love, and knowing that BIG LOVE is on its way,

Arielle

afterword

As someone who has been studying, practicing, and teaching the Law of Attraction for over forty years, I am thrilled to come across a book that so beautifully translates the universal principles of manifestation into an actionable plan for attracting a loving and fulfilling relationship. If you've applied the formula that Arielle has outlined here, you already know that the process of manifestation can be distilled down to a simple three-step equation: Step one is to **ask**. Step two is to **believe**. Step three is to **receive**.

The very fact that you've picked up this book is an indication that you are already asking. You're consciously aware of your desire to meet your soulmate and you are making the fulfillment of this desire a high priority. By writing your Soulmate List and creating a Treasure Map that visually represents your ideal relationship, you have identified the qualities and characteristics that are most important to you in a lover. You have *asked*, clearly and powerfully, for what you want. Now you must *believe* in your ability to attract it.

Since the movie phenomenon *The Secret* was released in 2006, hundreds of people have approached me to share a concern that goes something like this: *I've watched* The Secret *dozens of times. I've visualized the fulfillment of my desire in graphic detail. I've created a vision map so I can clearly picture the outcome I want to achieve. I meditate every day with the intention to manifest this goal, yet I still don't have what I want.* Regardless of the specific goal they are trying to achieve—whether it's losing weight, starting their own business, or meeting the man or woman of their dreams—my response is the same. "Stop watching the DVD," I tell them, "and get up off the couch!"

You see, it's not an accident that the last six letters of the word *attraction* spell ACTION! Meditating and visualizing that which we want to create is simply not enough. To get results in any area of our lives, we have to commit—in spirit, in mind, and in body. This means taking action . . . and this is where belief comes in. In the course of my travels, I meet a lot of committed people who consider themselves believers. They often go to great lengths to convince me of the power of their convictions. "I believe I have what it takes to succeed," they tell me. Or, "I believe I am worthy of experiencing deep and fulfilling love." But I'm going to suggest to you, as I do to them, that unless you are *in action*, unless you are regularly taking risks that expand your ability to allow love into your life, you do not yet believe that you will one day meet your soulmate. How do I know this? Because belief without action is really not belief.

Would you hesitate to throw a ball into the air out of fear that it will remain forever suspended in space? Of course not. You believe in the power of gravity to return the ball safely to your hands. This simple example illustrates that when you really believe in something, you act on it. Action is an essential part of the equation that simply cannot be skipped. In fact, there are two types of actions, both of which will bring you closer to your ultimate goal.

Some actions fall into the category of what I call "obvious actions." They operate under the common sense principle that says if you really want to succeed in any arena of life—be it in business, finances, or relationships—you first have to put yourself in the game. To borrow somewhat of a crude phrase, if you want to shoot a moose, you have to go where the moose are. If you want to meet a woman who shares your spiritual ideals, the obvious action would be to hang out at a church rather than at a bar. If you want to meet a great guy, the obvious action is to go places where guys go. Of course, it's possible to meet the man of your dreams while working as a nanny and living in a remote guesthouse—there is always the chance that you could fall head over heels in love with the mail carrier—but it's unlikely. By regularly placing yourself in environments where you are likely to encounter whatever it is you desire, you increase your odds and you strengthen the magnetic signal you're broadcasting to the Universe.

Next are what I call "inspired actions." Inspired actions are impulses that arise within you that don't appear to logically or directly correlate with your goal of falling in love. For example, you may be driving to work one morning when you have the sudden inclination to get off the freeway and stop for a latté at a favorite coffeehouse. While thoughts like these are easily dismissed as random or meaningless, the truth is that you have no idea where that impulse came from or where it may lead you if you choose to follow it. For all you know, your future wife or husband was guided by a similar urge and is sitting in that coffeehouse at the precise moment the thought crossed your mind.

By applying the formula outlined in this book, you have invited the potent forces of creation to partner with you in your pursuit of finding your soulmate. I can tell you from personal experience and from having shared these principles with literally hundreds of thousands of people that the Universe never declines such an invitation. It fulfills its end of the partnership by inspiring you to certain actions; your part of the deal is to act on the inspirations that arise from within, even if logically they don't make sense. Remember, every birth—be it the birth of a human being, a tree, a galaxy, or a passionate love affair—begins with a single creative impulse. This is why it's so imperative that you start following your hunches.

The final step in unlocking the equation of manifestation is to make yourself available to *receive* that which you've been asking for. To cultivate what the spiritual guides who call themselves Abraham refer to as the "receiving mode," we usually have to leave our preconceived expectations at the door. If you evaluate every person you meet through the filter of "is this the one?" you drastically limit the channels through which joy can flow into your life. Instead of approaching interactions with new people like a job interview, take a step back and you'll see that you have plenty of space in your heart and in your life to enjoy many different types of relationships. There are people who are fun to go bowling with and people who share your love of music or art. There are people who make you laugh and people with whom you can be incredibly creative and productive . . . my advice is to invite them all in. When you appreciate the unique contribution that each person brings into your life, you activate an internal state of abundance that attracts more wonderful experiences to you. On the other hand, when your vision is so narrow that you are only open to love if it comes through the conduit of your soulmate, you generate an internal state of lack and scarcity that actually repels the love you're seeking.

Just as expectations place conditions around the unconditional, rigid timelines are an attempt to place conditions around love, an experience that we all know unfolds in its own time. I am a huge advocate of goal-setting, but I've also come to understand that—especially when it comes to matters of the heart—it can be counterproductive to impose deadlines by which a goal "should" be realized. Of course you are eager to meet your soulmate and I guarantee that the Universe is not postponing your inevitable rendezvous just to torture you. It may appear this way to you in moments of desperation or loneliness, but that's only because our limited human perspective doesn't always allow us to see the whole picture. Think about the "Eye in the Sky" helicopters that circle overhead during rush hour to give commuters live updates on traffic conditions. As you tune in to your radio, the news report may recommend what seems like a longer route to your destination, but what you don't know is that by taking that alternate route, you'll avoid an accident up ahead and reach your goal with greater ease. You have released your desire to the infinite intelligence of the Universe and this force is, at this very moment, mapping out the best possible path for your fulfillment. And because its perspective is much broader than your own, it can envision a future for you that you may have never dared to envision for yourself.

The gestation period for a rabbit is two weeks; the same process takes two years for an elephant. Different dreams have different incubation periods before they are ready to hatch. Trust in your innate lovability, keep asking for what you want, act on your instincts, and allow yourself to receive love from all available sources. Have faith that the dream you hold in your heart is already a reality, and know that the person you are looking for is also looking for you.

—*Jack Canfield*

about the author

Arielle Ford has spent the past twenty-five years living and promoting consciousness through all forms of media. She is one of the founding partners of the Spiritual Cinema Circle, a DVD club dedicated to providing inspiring and uplifting movies. She is best known for helping to launch the careers of many bestselling self-help and spiritual authors including Deepak Chopra, Jach Canfield & Mark Victor Hansen of *Chicken Soup for the Soul*, Neale Donald Walsch, and many others. She is the author of seven books, including the *Hot Chocolate for the Mystical Soul* series. Arielle lives in La Jolla, California, with her husband and soulmate, Brian Hilliard, and their feline friends. Her websites include www.soulmatesecret.com and www.everythingyoushouldknow.com.

acknowledgments

I am blessed to be surrounded by many amazing people in my life who are both friends and business associates.

First and foremost, my deepest gratitude to the beautiful, smart, and always insightful Danielle Dorman for her editing skills. She is a shining star. Every writer should be lucky enough to have Danielle by his or her side.

To the amazingly talented Mike Koenigs, without whom there would not be www.soulmatekit.com (the inspiration for this book). His genius, generosity, and mind-boggling, multi-layered skill set as well as his grasp of technology stuff inspires me on a daily basis.

My heartfelt thanks to my friends who shared their personal stories: my incredible mother-in-law, Peggy Hilliard, and her soulmate John Morse, Marci Shimoff, Linda Sivertsen, Kathi Diamant, Drew Heriot and Jenny Keller, Peggy McColl, Stefanie Hartman, Sean Roach, Gayle Seminara-Mandel, Ken Foster, Colette Baron-Reid, and John Assaraf.

I am grateful to my delightful circle of friends for their on-going love and support: Carol Allen, Heide Banks and Howard Lazar, Reverend Laurie Sue Brockway, Christen Brown, Deepak and Rita Chopra, Nancy De Herrera, Vivian Glyck, Gay and Kathlyn Hendricks, Divina Infusino and Mark Schneider, Gloria Jones, Cynthia Kersey, Carla Picardi and Gofreddo Chiavelli, Carolyn Rangel, Becky Robbins, Faye Schell, Lisa Sharkey, Stephen and Lauren Simon, Jeremiah Sullivan, Renee Thomas, Jai Varadaraj, Marianne Wilson, and Scott and Shannon Peck.

To PR angel Jill Mangino, thanks, sister, for your love and support and for spreading the word!

To Shawne Mitchell, for contributing your wisdom and Feng Shui guidance, and to Louis Audet, whose Feng Sui wisdom has been an important guide in my life. To Scott Blum of DailyOm, my heartfelt thanks for your support and vision.

To my amazing co-workers at Gaiam. Who you are and what you do for the world changes lives for the better every single day.

This book would have never come to fruition without the love and support of my spectacular sister, Debbie Ford, whose work inspired some of the concepts in this book and who created the opportunity for my first public talk about soulmates on one of her cruises.

To the amazing dream team at HarperOne: Cynthia DiTiberio, Gideon Weil, Mark Tauber, Claudia Boutote, and Alison Petersen—thank you for making this experience fun and nearly effortless.

Big thanks to Marci Shimoff and Jack Canfield for your generous contributions and for always providing your love and support.

Deep love and appreciation goes to my mother, Sheila Fuerst, and my stepfather, Howard Fuerst, whose soulmate relationship was a daily reminder of what BIG LOVE really is.

Finally, my deepest gratitude goes to Amma, the Divine Mother, and to my soulmate, Brian Hilliard, who are both a daily expression of the highest manifestation of love.

the love mandala

To download additional copies of this mandala, please visit
www.soulmatesecret.com/mandala.